PROGRAMMING
IN occam 2

PROGRAMMING
IN occam 2

Alan Burns

University of Bradford

Addison-Wesley Publishing Company

Wokingham, England · Reading, Massachusetts · Menlo Park, California
New York · Don Mills, Ontario · Amsterdam · Bonn · Sydney
Singapore · Tokyo · Madrid · Bogota · Santiago · San Juan

the Instruction set

The Instruction Set Series
Published in collaboration with The Instruction Set Ltd.

Cover design by Crayon Design of Henley-on-Thames.
Typeset by Quorum Technical Services, Ltd.
Printed and bound in Great Britain by The Bath Press, Avon.

First printed 1988.

British Library Cataloguing in Publication Data

Burns, Alan, *1953–*
    Programming in Occam 2. — (The
    Instruction set series).
    1. occam (Computer program language)
    I. Title   II. Series
    005.13'3   QA76.73.03

    ISBN 0–201–17371–9

Library of Congress Cataloging in Publication Data

Burns, Alan, 1953–
    Programming in Occam 2.

    (The Instruction set)
    Bibliography: p.
    Includes index.
    1. occam2 (Computer program language)   2. Parallel
programming (Computer science)   I. Title.   II. Title:
Programming in Occam two.   III. Series.
QA76.73.0212B87   1987   005.13'3   87–24116

    ISBN 0–201–17371–9 (pbk.)

*This book is dedicated to the memory of
William G Hall (Bill), a close friend for a
number of years. It is in appreciation of his
many talents and gifts that this book is offered.*

Preface

Although a series of technical advances (in the last two decades) has significantly increased the execution speed of a standard Von-Neumann computer, there are insurmountable physical barriers that will inevitably restrict the power of the uniprocessor. The supercomputers of tomorrow will have to harness parallel computing if the insatiable appetite for faster and faster machines is to be even partially satisfied. The means by which the potential power of parallel processing may be captured is, however, a matter of much research, debate and experimentation.

Coupled to the development of multiprocessor and multicomputer systems has been the direct introduction into programming languages of the concept of concurrency. Not only have these languages had to deal with the possibility of parallel execution but they have had to recognize the fact that most computing applications (e.g. real-time systems) are inherently parallel in nature. Programming such applications in purely sequential languages has inevitably led to difficulties in terms of reliability, cost and maintainability. These sequential languages lack the expressive power to deal with the problem domain.

This book is concerned with one specific concurrent program language, occam 2. It also deals, to a lesser extent, with one means of harnessing parallel computing, namely transputers. Both of these developments are highly significant within the computing industry (and have been undertaken by the company INMOS).

A complete and comprehensive description of the language is given, with examples being used to illustrate all of the important features. No prior knowledge of concurrent programming (in general) is assumed. However, readers should have a good understanding of at least one high-level sequential programming language.

This book is aimed at professional software engineers, students of computer science (and other related disciplines) and application programmers. Contained within this last group are all those scientists and engineers who may wish to exploit occam and the transputer to solve problems that emerge within their own disciplines.

Occam 2, as its name suggests, is a language that has developed from earlier versions; the two most significant of which are preliminary occam and occam 1. Within this book the generic term 'occam' will be used to mean occam 2. Although the specification of occam 2 was only finalized in 1987, earlier versions of occam have been used in many large applications, and systems that use hundreds of transputers have been constructed. These early applications indicate that not only do multi-transputer systems give the increases in execution speed one would expect, but that occam is an appropriate language for expressing parallel activities and exploiting the potential power of the hardware.

The language itself is defined by documents that are internal to INMOS. There is no national or international standard. This will inevitably mean that versions of occam 2 will emerge that are not completely compatible with the material presented in this book.

Following an introduction, Chapter 2 looks, in detail, at the uses of concurrent programming and the inherent difficulties of providing inter-process communication. In order to understand fully the process model within occam it is necessary to consider first the wider topic of concurrent programming and to analyse the alternatives that are available when designing a language for expressing parallel activities.

Chapter 3 is the largest and perhaps most important chapter. It considers the basic structure of the language and describes most of the constructs that are provided. When considering occam it is important to realize that the language is not a sequential one to which concurrency has been added. The notion of process is fundamental to the design of occam, and communication between processes is seen to be at the same primitive level as the traditional assignment operation. This chapter is therefore called 'Occam Processes'.

Occam 2 is a strongly typed language, providing a range of predefined scalar types and the means by which arrays and records can be constructed. There is nothing novel about these provisions and the reader is assumed to be familiar with the concepts of type and data structure as they are used in Chapter 4. The version of occam described in this book, however, contains data structures, such as records, that may not be supported on all implementations.

The general issue of communicating data objects between processes is considered in Chapter 5. Between any two processes that wish to exchange data is defined an intermediary, known as a channel. Channels are defined with a protocol that specifies the type of the objects that are allowed to be passed down that channel. Such protocols can be a simple type, a sequence of types or a variant. Variants protocols are used to allow two processes to communicate a variety of objects without having to use a number of different channels.

The main form of modularity within occam is the procedure. Chapter 6 describes the occam PROC and the associated parameter passing model. This model is based on the concept of abbreviation. Examples of PROCs are given and some important issues about the design of occam programs are discussed. Functions are supported and these are also illustrated in this chapter.

Chapters 7 and 8 are concerned with the transputer. Firstly the transputer itself is described and then in Chapter 8 the implementation of occam on the transputer is considered. This illustrates the close association between the transputer and the language. Occam has been designed so that an efficient implementation is possible and, more significantly, the transputer's basic architecture and instruction set have been chosen so that the most effective means of programming the device is in a high level concurrent programming language – not assembler or machine code!

Specifying input and output within high level languages is always non-trivial and many languages choose a mechanism that is at variance with the basic model of the language (cf. Pascal). Occam allows specially defined channels to pass data into (or out of) the program. This provides an adequate, if not very powerful, interface between the program and its environment. More significantly, occam also provides for the direct programming of the necessary low-level interfaces between external devices and controlling software. This is described in Chapter 9.

One of the attractive features of occam is that it has been designed with formal specification techniques in mind. Although a formal specification of the semantics of the language is beyond the scope of this book, one of the benefits of having a formal basis to the language is that transformation laws can be defined. A transformation law expresses an equivalence between two fragments of occam code; if they are equivalent then one can be exchanged for the other. This technique by which occam programs are transformed (to, for example, increase their parallelism) is discussed in Chapter 10. By considering occam laws not only are transformation techniques introduced, but the semantics of the language constructs are re-emphasized and further programming techniques are introduced.

Finally, in the last chapter, a comparison is made between occam and the important and (relatively) new language Ada. This material illustrates how two concurrent programming languages, which superficially have similar structures, are in fact, in detail, quite distinct.

The material presented in this book reflects the author's experiences in writing and giving industrial courses on occam and on the transputer. These courses are given on behalf of The Instruction Set. Occam is now studied by most computer science students in the UK and much of the material in this book forms part of final year and MSc courses at the University of Bradford (UK).

Braille copies

Braille copies of this book, on paper or Versabraille cassette, can be made available. Enquiries should be addressed to Dr Alan Burns, Postgraduate School of Studies in Computing, University of Bradford, BRADFORD, West Yorkshire, BD7 1DP, UK.

Acknowledgements

It would be impossible to thank, other than in a general way, all those who have helped me construct this book on occam. I must however explicitly mention Paul Luker who was originally the co-author of this work before he left the University of Bradford. The attractions of better prospects and facilities caused a move from the UK to California. It is an indictment of those responsible for funding higher education and research in the UK that a move abroad seems to be only way one can satisfactorily continue one's work.

Throughout the production of this book I have been grateful for the full cooperation that has been given me by INMOS. In particular I would wish to express my thanks to Michael Poole.

A number of people have made useful comments on earlier versions of the manuscript. Two people deserve specific mention and thanks: David Crowe and Andy Wellings.

The code presented in this book has been checked on a Beta-2 release version of the occam 2 compiler. I must thank Gordon Manson and the University of Sheffield Computer Science Department for providing me with access to this compiler.

Finally I would like gratefully to acknowledge the efforts and achievements of the designers of occam (David May and his team); they have provided us with a most powerful tool.

Contents

CHAPTER 1

Introduction

The emergence of VLSI technology has enabled and encouraged the widespread use of multiprocessor and multicomputer systems. It is now possible to construct, as a single device, a powerful microcomputer with memory, processor and communications. These microcomputers can then be linked together to give high performance systems with arbitrary topologies. Indeed they can be considered as the 'building blocks' for such systems in the same way that logic gates can be combined to form digital systems (May and Taylor, 1984).

This changing structure of computer hardware has put pressure on language designers to provide the primitives necessary to allow programmers to express parallelism directly within their programs. These primitives must not only be easy to use and have adequate expressive power but they must also be implementable in a way that harnesses the potential power of these multiprocessor architectures (whilst giving acceptable performance on single processor systems). Occam is one such language; its design has been closely associated with the development of the transputer and yet it is an abstract language that has the dual role of being an implementation language and a design formalism. Although linked with the transputer, the importance of occam goes beyond its implementation on any particular hardware system. It represents the culmination of many years of research effort that has been centred on the CSP language (Hoare, 1978, 1985). The result of this is a concurrent programming language that is simple, elegant and powerful.

The name occam was chosen in recognition of this simplicity. William of Occam, a 14th century philosopher, is responsible for the adage (known as Occam's razor) that: 'Entities are not to be multiplied beyond necessity'. This is normally used as a plea to keep things simple. Although the present definition of occam (the one described in this book) is clearly not as simple as earlier versions (INMOS, 1984), it is nevertheless much less complex than other concurrent programming languages such as Ada (Burns, 1985).

1

1.1   The nature of concurrency

In the above paragraphs occam (and Ada) were described as concurrent, rather than parallel, programming languages. The terms **concurrent** and **parallel** have similar but distinct meanings and it is important that they are not confused. Two entities are said to be executing in parallel if at some instant in time both are actually executing. Entities are described as concurrent if they have the potential for executing in parallel. A concurrent programming language will therefore have more than one distinct thread of control. Objects that could execute in parallel are directly represented. This can be compared with sequential languages such as FORTRAN, COBOL and Pascal in which there is only a single thread of control.

The most flexible mode of concurrency is known as MIMD (Multiple Instruction Multiple Data). This implies that the distinct threads of control can be executing different instructions and manipulating different data structures. MIMD concurrency can be compared with other more restricted forms of concurrency such as vector processing or SIMD (Single Instruction Multiple Data). The objects that can execute simultaneously within a MIMD framework are usually known as **processes**; another term often used is **task**. In some concurrent programming languages processes can only be defined at the top level; other languages allow for their hierarchical structuring (in which case there is a parent–child relationship between processes in the hierarchy). Some languages allow for dynamic process creation (while the program is executing), others will only support a static set. The process itself can be large and complex like a disk controller or, at the other extreme, a single statement may represent a process.

The representation of processes, within a language, takes many forms, as do the semantic rules that govern when a process should start executing and when it can terminate. In addition, a concurrent programming language will need to support some means by which processes can communicate data and synchronize their executions. These issues are discussed in Chapter 2. Finally some method by which a process can delay itself will need to be supported. In real-time systems a process will often wish to be delayed until some future event has taken place. This must be done in an efficient way that does not waste processor cycles or lead to unnecessary communications.

The implementation of a system of processes may take, in general, one of three forms.

1. All processes run on a single processor.

2. Each process runs on its own processor and all processes have access to common memory.

3. Each process runs on its own processor and there is no shared memory. Processors are linked by a communication network.

Hybrids of these three structures are also possible. For example there could be a collection of processors, some of which have shared memory, and upon each processor a number of processes may execute. Note that only in cases (2) and (3) are processes actually executing in parallel. However they are all concurrent systems.

After coming into existence a process's life-history can be defined in terms of three primary states: **executing**, **executable** and **suspended**. A process is suspended if it is delayed (most synchronization primitives can lead to delay). This state is also known as **blocked**, and **unrunnable**. If it is not suspended then a process can either be executing, if there is a processor available, or be able to execute (but be prohibited from doing so by the lack of a processor).

With earlier languages aimed at real-time programming such as JOVIAL, CORAL66 and RTL/2 the support for the above process states, and the interprocess communication, was undertaken by an underlying operating system. Modern languages do not require any such support; however the compiler will generate a **run-time system** that will manage the queues of suspended and executable processes. If at any time there are not enough processors for the executable processes (this will usually be the case) then the run-time system will need to schedule the executable work. When moving from running one process to running another, the run-time system must also cater for state changes, which it does using a procedure known as a **context switch**. This will involve storing the volatile environment of the current running process and restoring the corresponding environment of the process that is due to run next.

1.2 Occam and the transputer

Although occam is an abstract programming language its development has been closely associated with that of the transputer. (Both have been designed by INMOS.) The transputer is a programmable VLSI device containing communication links for point-to-point inter-transputer connections. Occam's model of concurrency has been strongly influenced by the need to provide the same programming techniques on a single transputer and a network of transputers. This enables a programmer to be, essentially, unconcerned about the final implementation scheme chosen for the program. It can be defined, coded and verified prior to a decision being made on configuration. Such a decision (known as post-fragmentation) may favour running on a low-cost single transputer or a high performance multi-transputer system.

The transputer's effect on the design of occam is nevertheless minor when compared with occam's influence over the hardware development. Although there is a minimal instruction set (see Chapter 7) the lowest level at which the transputer will normally be programmed is occam; it is an occam machine. In particular, many of the functions of the run-time system are supported, directly, in the hardware. Process suspension, scheduling, queue manipulation and context switching are all undertaken efficiently by the transputer. This should make it possible to implement time-critical applications in occam on the transputer.

In terms of a concurrent programming language the link between occam and the transputer should not be considered too strongly. Occam is not a peculiar assembly language for an esoteric piece of hardware. It is a general purpose language based on sound theoretical study. This book is about occam, not the transputer. The transputer is considered here only as an example of how occam can be implemented. This is a significant topic when compared with languages like Ada where an efficient implementation has been difficult to obtain (Burns, 1985). The execution of occam on a transputer network is considered in Chapter 8.

1.3   The uses of occam

Concurrent programming languages, in general, have two broad classifications of use.

1. They provide for the direct programming of applications with concurrent objects.
2. They provide for the direct representation of objects which will execute in parallel on multiprocessor hardware.

The first classification is concerned, primarily, with embedded systems, where the computer (hardware and software) forms part of some larger engineering system. The computer will monitor, and probably control, the behaviour of this larger system. It does this by exchanging data with its environment. A typical engineering system will have a number of distinct devices that exist 'in parallel'. If the software of the computer system is written in a sequential language then the mapping of the family of device controllers onto a sequential program is unnatural, and therefore error-prone, difficult to maintain and unreliable. With a concurrent programming language the parallel objects of the environment can be coupled with processes in the software. Programs are easier to write and have increased expressive power. Even if the execution of this program takes place on a single processor (i.e. pseudo-parallel execution) the benefits in terms of the software engineering are significant.

By comparison, the second class of application is concerned with execution. It is understandably difficult for a compiler to generate code, that can be executed sensibly, in parallel, from a sequential program. Algorithms that can exploit multiprocessor execution must be represented (and implemented) in a language that will allow for the expression of parallelism. The resulting programs are very different from their sequential counterparts and may actually be inefficient if executed on a single processor.

These two quite distinct uses of concurrent programming languages are not entirely complementary. The language SIMULA, for example, was designed to cater for class one; as a result it uses a form of process representation, known as coroutines, that cannot effectively be executed in parallel. Only relatively recently have multiprocessor and multicomputer architectures become feasible and therefore the needs of class two are now beginning to be realized. Because of occam's association with the transputer it has a clear role in the implementation of parallel algorithms. Although this is not to the exclusion of the more traditional use of a concurrent programming language.

Where both types of application come together is in the use of multiprocessor embedded systems. In order to obtain the required performance (in terms of speed and/or reliability), an increasing number of real-time systems find it is necessary to use more than one processor. Physical distribution within an embedded system is also becoming more commonplace. Fortunately the processes defined to model external objects are usually those that it is most sensible to execute in parallel.

Occam, and in many cases the transputer, has already been analysed for its use in many different domains. Some of the envisaged uses are: sorting and searching algorithms, fast fourier transforms, signal processing, digital differential analyser, image processing, image display, high speed logical inference engine, industrial control, process automation, simulation and data acquisition. In addition many parallel algorithms are described in terms of a systolic implementation (Kung, 1982), for example matrix multiplication; occam is able to express such algorithms easily.

As well as its role as a concurrent programming language occam can also be used as a normal high level language for system software. Indeed INMOS have used occam to write a compiler for occam.

CHAPTER 2

Interprocess
Communication

The major difficulties associated with concurrent programming arise from
process interaction. Processes are rarely independent of each other and
there is a need to transfer data, and synchronize actions, between related
processes. The method by which interprocess communication is supported
within a programming language is the subject of much debate and many
different models exist (see Andrews and Schneider, 1983). This chapter
will consider some of these models and will describe the inherent problems
associated with interprocess communication. The motivation for the design
of occam will emerge from this discussion.

2.1   Synchronization and data communication

Data communication between processes, in general, is based upon either
shared variables or message passing. Shared variables are objects to which
two or more processes have access; by writing to, or reading from these
variables, data can be passed from one process to another. Message
passing involves the explicit exchange of data between the partners
involved in the communication. Associated with the act of data communication is the concept of process synchronization. Although processes
execute essentially independently, there are situations where it is necessary
for two or more processes to coordinate their executions. For example, in
order for one process to have received a message it is necessary for some
other process first to have sent that message. Synchronization can be
defined simply as one process possessing knowledge about the state of
another process. In most cases data communication will necessitate an act
of synchronization; indeed the occam model is based on a single primitive
(the rendezvous) which combines communication and synchronization.

   With languages based on shared variables an important class of
synchronization is mutual exclusion. This is needed to stop simultaneous
access to shared objects (usually resources of the system) in situations

6

important synchronization is condition synchronization; this is necessary when a process wishes to perform an operation that can only sensibly, or safely, be performed if another process has undertaken some action or is in some defined state. Condition synchronization can be supported with shared variables or message passing.

The use of buffers to decrease the coupling between active processes is a common feature of systems written in a concurrent programming language. They also illustrate well the forms of synchronization just discussed. If the buffer itself, and its associated pointers, are open to concurrent access then it will be necessary to provide mutual exclusion to give a reliable implementation. Moreover two condition synchronizations also apply to buffers; these are needed to stop a process reading from an empty buffer or writing to a full one.

2.2 Shared variables

Data communication based on shared variables is available in many languages, although as will be indicated later, occam does not employ this mechanism other than in a very restricted form. The use of shared variables is easy and usually efficient; however, they suffer from three significant difficulties.

1. Although the processes have access to a shared variable the processors on which they execute may not have shared memory.
2. Multiple-update difficulties necessitate that such variables be protected from uncontrolled access.
3. The use of shared variables complicates the formal model of the semantics of the language and makes program verification much more difficult.

In order to illustrate the second point a simple example will be given. Let X be an integer variable that can be accessed by two processes, P1 and P2. Consider the following assignment:

```
X := X + 1
```

On most computers this assignment could be implemented in three stages.

1. Copy value of X into some register.
2. Add 1 to value on register.
3. Store value on register at the address for X.

If P1 and P2 both execute such an assignment then interference between the two sets of actions can lead to an unexpected result. For example, let X be initially zero and let the interaction between P1 and P2 be such that the following interleaving is executed:

1. P2 copies value of X(=0) into its register.
2. P1 copies value of X(=0) into its register.
3. P1 adds 1 to its register.
4. P1 stores value of X(=1).
5. P2 adds 1 to its register.
6. P2 stores value of X(=1).

Rather than obtain the value 2 the result is only 1.

This difficulty with shared variables has resulted in many different language constructs being proposed. These include semaphores (Dijkstra, 1968 a, b), critical control regions (Hoare, 1972; Brinch Hansen, 1972, 1973 a, 1981) and monitors (Dijkstra, 1968 b; Brinch Hansen, 1973 b; Hoare, 1974). Occam allows read only access to shared variables and has thereby removed one of the most contentious areas of concurrent programming.

2.3 Models of message passing

If shared variables are not to be used then a language must employ message passing. One process will SEND a message, another process will WAIT for it to arrive. Surprisingly the definition of these SEND and WAIT commands can be based on a variety of independent factors leading to many different models of these message passing primitives.

The first and most significant factor concerns the behaviour of the process that executes the SEND. If this process is delayed until the corresponding WAIT is executed then the message passing is said to be **synchronous**. Alternatively, if the SEND process continues executing arbitrarily then the communication is termed **asynchronous**. The drawback with the asynchronous method is that the receiving process cannot know anything about the present state of the calling process; it only has information on some previous state. Indeed it is even possible that the calling process has terminated before its message is read. In addition, the calling process does not know, directly, if the message sent has ever been received.

Where a reply message is generated it is possible for the process executing a synchronous SEND to be delayed further until this reply is received. This structure, known as **remote invocation**, is used in Ada (Burns, *et al.*, 1987).

Another important issue in the design of a message based programming language is how destinations and sources are designated. The simplest form is for unique names to be given to all processes in the system; a SEND command will then directly name the destination processes:

```
SEND <message> TO <process-name>
```

A symmetric form for the receiving process would be:

```
WAIT <message> FROM <process-name>
```

This symmetric form requires the receiver to know the name of any process liable to send it a message. By comparison an asymmetric form may be used if the receiver is only interested in the existence of a message rather than from where it came:

```
WAIT <message>
```

This asymmetric form is particularly useful when the nature of the relationship between the two processes fits the client/server paradigm. The server process renders some utility to any client process that requires it (though usually only one client at a time). Clearly the client must name the server when sending a request message but the server need not know the identity of the caller unless a reply message must be sent.

Where the unique naming of all processes is inappropriate a language may define intermediaries (usually called mailboxes or channels) that are named by both partners in the communication.

```
SEND <message> TO <mailbox>
WAIT <message> FROM <mailbox>
```

Again there are a number of forms that a mailbox may take; a single mailbox could be defined to be used by many readers and many writers, one reader and many writers or one reader and one writer. Moreover it may be structured to pass information in both directions or in only one. Finally the message itself could be complex like a structured data type or simple such as a 16-bit word.

With all of these message structures the receiving process, by executing a WAIT, commits itself to the synchronization and will be suspended if there is no message immediately available. This is, in general, too restrictive; the receiving process may wish to choose between a number of possible message sources. Within this structure it may also wish, temporarily, to restrict the sources over which it wishes to exercise this choice. These two properties lead to a language structure in which a process selects one of a set of alternative input messages, each of which may be guarded to impose a condition synchronization. For example, if the buffer process mentioned earlier communicated with its clients via messages then guards could be used to inhibit the processing of PLACE messages when the buffer is full or a TAKE message when it is empty. During normal operation (i.e. when the buffer is neither empty nor full) the buffer process will deal with either PLACE or TAKE messages depending on which is outstanding.

2.4   The occam channel

The above section has illustrated the wide range of message passing models that it is possible to construct when designing a language that is not going to base its data communication on shared variables. Occam uses a single straightforward structure that encompasses both ease of programming and ease of implementation. Following the design of CSP, a synchronous communication method (the rendezvous) was chosen that combines, in a single primitive, the needs of data communication and synchronization. This is a logical model to choose as it is arguable that communication without synchronization is rarely useful and that synchronization must, conceptually, imply some form of communication.

Occam's rendezvous is built upon the use of an intermediary which is known as a **channel**. Two factors have particularly influenced this choice.

1. Occam incorporates an exhaustive view of concurrency, programs consist of a large number of processes and it would be inconvenient to have to name them all. Indirect naming allows processes to be anonymous.

2. Modifications to occam programs are easier to accommodate if the communication between processes takes place via an explicitly defined intermediary.

The channel is unidirectional and can only be used by one calling process and one called process. Other characteristics of the channel have also been influenced by the need to associate a channel with a link between adjacent transputers.

The commands for reading and writing to a channel have a simple (if somewhat terse) syntactical form. To write to a channel ch the value contained in the variable X the following simple process is executed:

```
ch ! X
```

The symbol ! indicates output.

To read from this channel (in another process) into a variable Y requires the execution of:

```
ch ? Y
```

Here, the symbol ? is synonymous with input.

As the communication is synchronous, the first process to execute one of the above commands will be suspended until the other process 'catches up'. When and only when both processes are ready to communicate will data pass from X to Y. Both processes will then proceed, independently and concurrently.

It was indicated earlier that with a message-based communication system it is necessary to provide a command that will allow a server process to make a guarded choice between a number of possible communication sources. This command in occam is known as the ALT statement and is discussed in Section 3.6. The implementation of a channel either on a single processor or between processors is considered in Chapter 8.

2.5   Deadlocks and indefinite postponements

Before proceeding to consider the occam language in detail it is necessary to discuss some other concepts that affect interprocess communication. These concern the behaviour of the system once it is executing. The most serious condition to arise in a working system is **deadlock**. This occurs when a group of processes is in a state in which it is impossible for any of them to proceed. Consider two occam processes P1 and P2 that wish to exchange some data; let chan1 and chan2 be two channels. The following code will work correctly:

```
       P1                            P2
   chan1 ! A                     chan1 ? X
   chan2 ? B                     chan2 ! Y
```

For example, assume that P1 reaches this code before P2; it will be delayed by attempting to write to chan1. When P2 arrives it will read from chan1 (thereby freeing P1) and become suspended on the output action on chan2. P1 will proceed to read from chan2 and in doing so P2 will become executable again. The data transfer is complete (A to X and Y to B) and both processes are active.

However the following will inevitably lead to both processes being suspended indefinitely:

```
       P1                            P2
   chan1 ! A                     chan2 ! Y
   chan2 ? B                     chan1 ? X
```

P1 cannot proceed until P2 has read from chan1; P2 cannot do this until it has written to chan2, which it cannot do until P1 has read from chan2.

The testing of software rarely removes other than the most obvious deadlocks; they can occur infrequently but with devastating results. It is not practicable to design a concurrent program language in which deadlocks are impossible to construct nor is it likely that compilers will be intelligent enough to find them. It is thus necessary for the designers of a program to illustrate, or prove, that the possibility of deadlock has been removed from their software. Various design methods can assist in this task. In particular CSP (Hoare, 1985) is a formalism that can be used to prove absence (or detect presence) of potential deadlock.

With deadlock all affected processes are suspended indefinitely. A similarly acute condition is where a collection of processes are inhibited from proceeding but are still executing. This situation is known as **livelock**. A typical example would be a collection of interacting processes stuck in loops from which they cannot proceed but in which they are doing no useful work.

A less severe, though still significant, condition is **indefinite postponement** (sometimes called **lockout** or **starvation**). This is where a process, although it is able to proceed, finds that it is not actually doing so. For example, if processes are given priorities then a low priority process may never gain access to a busy resource. Even if the postponement is not indefinite, but merely indeterminate, making assertions about the program's behaviour may still be impossible.

An alternative way of looking at indefinite postponement is to consider the inverse property. A system of processes is said to possess **liveness** if all requests made by processes are eventually met. A stronger characteristic would be **fairness**, but it is difficult to give a precise meaning to this. Structures that use a first-in, first-out queue or a round-robin algorithm can be considered to be fair. It is useful if the run-time system that supports the concurrent execution of processes implements a fair scheduling algorithm, at least at each priority level.

CHAPTER 3

Occam Processes

The basic model for an occam program is a network of communicating processes. Communication is via defined channels with each process within the program performing a sequence of actions which may proceed indefinitely. If a process has a finite existence then it will eventually either terminate (the normal course) or STOP (this usually signifies an error condition). A process may contain other processes so that a hierarchical structure is supported; indeed a complete occam program is considered, at the topmost level, to be a single process.

Within the sequence of statements that a process performs, data will be manipulated. Occam supports a number of data types; discussion of these is, however, postponed until the next chapter so that attention can be focused here on the structure of an occam program. In order to give example programs a correct form, integer and Boolean variables, constants and expressions will be used where necessary. These are defined as follows:

```
INT i,j,k:    -- integer variables
BOOL finished:   -- Boolean variable
VAL INT Top IS 10:   -- integer constant Top

i + j       -- integer expression
i > j       -- Boolean expression
```

Each statement in a program normally occupies a single line. If it is necessary to continue a statement on a second (or subsequent) line then the line must be broken after an expression operator (or similar) and the new line must be indented by at least as much as the first one. Program comments are introduced by the character pair --, they are terminated by the end of that line.

At any instant a typical occam program will have a number of processes that could execute simultaneously. In recognition of this independent relationship we say that the processes are concurrent and it is useful, conceptually, to visualize each process as having its own logical processor. In reality many processes will be sharing each available processor, but this knowledge rarely impinges itself upon the software developer. As was discussed in the previous chapter all communication between processes must use channels as intermediaries. It is however acceptable for two or more processes to reference a constant or a variable as long as no process attempts to update this variable. In some implementations even this read only facility may be denied if the processes are destined to execute on different processors. This is one of the few situations in which it is necessary during software design to be aware of the likely final distribution of the system. The maintenance of programs moved from one implementation to another may find this restriction significant, although the existence of formal transformation techniques may lessen this difficulty (see Chapter 10).

An occam process can take many different forms ranging from a complete program to a single simple assignment. The following classification describes the process types found in general use:

- primitive process,
- block,
- constructor,
- procedure instance (see Chapter 6).

This description of occam processes is analogous to viewing, say, an Ada program as being made up of simple statements, compound statements, blocks, control and while statements, and procedure calls.

3.1   Occam names

Before consideration of occam processes it is necessary to discuss, briefly, the basic syntactical structure of occam code. A **name** in occam consists of a sequence of alphabetic characters, decimal digits and dots (.); the first symbol must be an alphabetic character. The use of dot helps to improve readability; examples of valid occam names are:

```
Maximum.Value
Start.Position
Input.Channel
First.Time.Element
SET.VALUE
clock
in1
fred.42
```

There is a style convention amongst occam programmers to use an upper case letter at the beginning of each word that makes up a name. The alphabetic characters include both the upper case (A...Z) and lower case (a...z) sequences. Contained within the full occam character set are the usual special characters:

```
! " # & ' ( ) * + , - . / : ; < = > ? [ ]
```

An implementation may also include other characters for use in strings and character constants. Certain unprintable ASCII characters are accessed via the meta-character asterisk:

*c	carriage return
*n	newline
*t	horizontal tab
*s	space
*'	quotation mark
*"	double quotation mark
**	asterisk

All names in occam are case sensitive; therefore FRED is a different object from Fred and they could both exist in the same program, although this is not recommended. Reserved words (see Appendix A for a complete list) have to be in upper case.

3.2   Primitive processes

Occam supports five primitive processes: STOP, SKIP, assignment, input and output. STOP is a process that has no action but which never terminates. Its effect therefore is to inhibit any parent process from continuing. This action is clearly quite drastic and a process will usually only execute a STOP in recognition of some error condition. Some program structures also default to STOP when they are used erroneously (for example numerical overflow when evaluating an expression).

The SKIP process is the inverse of STOP although it also has no effect. SKIP is a process that is always ready to execute and which terminates immediately. It is the null process and is used with certain syntactical forms to indicate, explicitly, that no action is required.

An assignment in occam has the form:

```
V := e
```

where V is a variable and e is an expression of the same type. It is important to appreciate that this familiar assignment is viewed, in occam, as a process in its own right. Hence it is pertinent to ask when does it terminate? An expression is a collection of variables, constants, operators and function calls. Functions are however restricted in structure; they cannot have side-effects and cannot give rise to internal processes. The process that executes an assignment cannot therefore be delayed and will normally terminate immediately, although, as mentioned above, an error condition may force the assignment process to STOP.

One of the novel and important features of occam is that it views communication at the same primitive level as assignment. The occam channel was described in the previous chapter; the symbol ? denotes input and ! output:

```
ch ! e    -- output

ch ? V    -- input
```

where ch is a channel, e is again an expression and V is a variable (the variable and the expression being of the same type). As the message passing is synchronized the output process will only terminate when there is an associated input process acting on the same channel. (Similarly, input will only terminate when there is an output.) The effect of this rendezvous is to have executed:

```
V := e
```

where V is in one process and e in another. It is thus appropriate to classify assignment, input and output together.

The discerning reader will have noticed that there are no semicolons acting as either statement terminators or statement separators. Each line of an occam program can contain only one statement (process); it must however start in the correct column (see below). If a statement must continue onto the following line then it may do so as long as it starts at a column position equal or to the right of the previous line.

3.3   Blocks and channels

A block process is a specification followed by a process. This recursive definition provides the usual block structure in which any number of objects can be declared prior to an area of the program in which these objects are used. Blocks may be contained within blocks and the usual scope rules apply (i.e. an inner declaration hides an outer one for the same name). It is however always possible to substitute new names into a program so that no single name is specified more than once. If this has been done the program is said to have a **canonical** form.

The only object declarations of interest in this chapter are the channels. These are specified by placing a list of names after the specification of the channel type; the list is terminated by a colon (as are all declarations), for example:

```
CHAN OF P C:
CHAN OF P C1,C2,primes,print:
```

The clause P in these declarations is the protocol associated with the use of these channels. These indicate the type of data that can use that channel; a full description of protocols is given in Chapter 5. The simplest protocol involves the passing of single integer values; this will be the form assumed in this chapter. A channel C with this protocol is defined as follows:

```
CHAN OF INT C:
```

A vector of channels is defined by stating the size of the array in square brackets:

```
[32]CHAN OF INT C,OUT:
```

This declares two vectors both having 32-channel elements; these elements are numbered from zero:

```
C[0] ! a + b    -- output a + b through channel C[0]
```

As processes in occam are not named it is impossible to specify which two processes may use any defined channel. Usage will therefore complete a channel's specification and a compiler is able to recognize and reject misuse – i.e. more than one process using the channel for input (or output).

The occam rendezvous is a single primitive that combines synchronization and data communication. In the situation where only synchronization is required a dummy piece of data must still be communicated. This could lead to confusion for someone reading the program at a later date. A useful program idiom to apply in these circumstances is to input a constant of the name Any and to output to a variable also of that name:

```
C ! Any
```

```
C ? Any
```

If this convention is followed it will be clear when a synchronization is being used in which the data communicated is irrelevant.

In Chapter 9 the methods by which an occam program interacts with its environment are described. However, for readers who have access to an occam system and are developing code concurrently with reading this book (in order to consolidate their understanding!) it is worth noting here how an occam program communicates with a keyboard and screen. In keeping with most high level languages the details of I/O are implementation dependent. The general model is of certain channels linking the program with its environment. One such channel may enable an output process to pass characters to the screen. Another channel could be used to read characters from a keyboard. All such channels have the property that, within the program, they are either written to (and not read from) or read from (and not written to). They are defined by placing the channel at a particular location:

```
CHAN OF INT Keyboard:
PLACE Keyboard AT 2:
CHAN OF ANY Screen:
PLACE Screen AT 1:
```

Note, the protocol given with these channels is INT for keyboard (the value obtained is the ASCII representation of the character typed) and ANY for screen. The use of 'type' ANY is described in Chapter 5.

The value after the AT is implementation dependent; the names chosen, Keyboard and Screen, are not significant (merely appropriate). On some implementations the definition of these channels will have been done by the development environment. Predefined procedures that use these channels for outputting integers, characters, reals, etc. may also be supported.

Finally in this section, the special TIMER 'channels' will be introduced. These return the value of the local real-time clock. A TIMER is declared in the normal way (for a channel):

```
TIMER Big.Ben:
```

Any number of TIMERs can be defined but each one is restricted to the use of only one process.

A TIMER has the characteristic that it is always ready to output (i.e. a process cannot be delayed by inputting from a TIMER). Obviously only read actions on TIMERs are allowed:

```
Big.Ben ? Time
```

The meaning of the value returned from a TIMER is implementation dependent. It is not in the form of a clock giving time in hours, seconds or microseconds; rather it is a simple integer (INT) value that is incremented regularly by the host hardware.

In order to delay a process until some time, in the future, the following structure is provided:

```
Big.Ben ? AFTER T
```

The process that executes this action on the TIMER Big.Ben will be delayed until the value of the real-time clock is greater or equal to T. That is, T is an absolute value not a relative time period from the present. Examples of the use of this delay facility will be given later when the necessary data types and operators have been discussed.

The time that a process is delayed for is, inevitably, only approximate. It cannot be less than required but it could be more. For example if two processes, running on the same processor, both delay to the same time in the future then clearly only one can be actually woken up at that time. The other must be executed later. Alternatively they may both be further delayed due to the scheduling algorithm used by the implementation. To emphasize this necessary lack of precision when delaying a process the reserved word AFTER is used in the syntax.

3.4 Constructors

Constructors provide the glue for grouping together primitive processes. Five distinct constructors are provided: SEQ, PAR, WHILE, IF and ALT. With each of these (apart from WHILE) a **replicator** can be attached to give an extra dimension to the structure. SEQ, WHILE and IF are familiar high level language features and they will be discussed first in this section. Then PAR, which enables concurrent processes to be defined, and ALT will be considered.

3.4.1 SEQ

SEQ provides for the sequential execution of a collection of processes:

```
SEQ
    A := 4          -- for some integer A
    B := A + 42     -- for some integer B
    out ! B         -- for some channel out
```

The collection can be of any size and is expressed as one subprocess per line beginning in the column under the Q in SEQ. There is no need to indicate explicitly the end of the SEQ construct, a change in the indentation of the program (to the left) is interpreted as the end. Each subprocess within the construct must terminate before the next process can execute. The SEQ is itself a process that will terminate when and only when the last subprocess has terminated.

The syntax for a SEQ can be expressed formally as follows (a complete description of occam's syntax is given in Appendix B).

```
sequence = SEQ
              {process}
```

The notation *{process}* means 'a list of zero or more processes on separate lines'. We have already described the different types of processes available in occam:

```
process =   SKIP
          | STOP
          | action
          | construction
          | block
          | instance  -- of PROC
action =    assignment
          | input
          | output
block = specification
        scope
scope = process
```

Specifications are dealt with in the next chapter.

As was indicated above a construction can have one of five forms:

```
construction =   sequence
               | conditional
               | loop
               | parallel
               | alternation
```

3.4.2 WHILE

To execute a sequence a number of times requires the use of a WHILE constructor or a replicator. The WHILE constructor acts on a single process, re-executing it each time the associated Boolean expression evaluates to TRUE:

```
loop = WHILE Boolean
         process
```

For example:

```
WHILE A<0
  in ? A
```

In this example a number of objects will be read down channel in until a non-negative value is encountered; at this point the WHILE construct will terminate. Note again that the subprocess is indicated by a two character position indent. To execute a sequence of statements within the while loop it is necessary to combine a WHILE with a SEQ:

```
INT A:
WHILE A <= 1024
  SEQ
    in ? A
    A := A * A
    out ! A
```

Here the square of A is passed on to channel out until a value greater than 32 (or less than −32) is taken from in. With this code A must be tested prior to the first value being input; this should be made secure by giving an initial low value to A:

```
INT A:
SEQ
  A := 0
  WHILE A < 1024
    SEQ
      in ? A
      A := A * A
      out ! A
```

Alternatively the statements could be rearranged so that the first input takes place before the WHILE:

```
INT A:
SEQ
  in ? A
  A := A * A
  WHILE A < 1024
    SEQ
      out ! A
      in ? A
      A := A * A
  out ! A
```

Note that the last line is needed so that the final value is passed on.

Formally the loop process can be defined (recursively) by the following relationship, in which b is a Boolean expression and p is any occam process:

```
WHILE b = IF
    p         b
              SEQ
                p
                WHILE b
                  p
```

```
          NOT b
          SKIP
```

The IF process is considered below.

3.4.3   Replicators

A replicator is employed to duplicate a component process a number of times. It can be used in conjunction with either a SEQ, PAR, IF or ALT constructor and has the general form:

```
replicator = name = base FOR count

base = expression

count = expression
```

where *name* is an INT variable defined by the replicator; *base* is the initial value of this variable and *count* is the number of times the replicator is applied. (It follows that *base* and *count* must be of type INT.) With each replication the variable is given a new value: *base, base + 1, base + 2, ..., base + count − 1.*

The use of the replicator with a SEQ provides the usual 'for' loop found in most conventional languages. For example the following code transmits the integers 0, 1, 2, ..., 9 down channel CNT:

```
SEQ i = 0 FOR 10
   CNT ! i
```

A replicated SEQ can only be applied on a single subprocess, to execute a collection of subprocesses requires a further constructor:

```
SEQ
   total := 0
   SEQ i = 1 FOR N
     SEQ
       CNT ? temp
       total := total + temp
   SUM ! total
```

Here the code outputs through channel SUM the sum of the first N integers read down channel CNT.

If the *count* value is initially zero then the replicated SEQ becomes equivalent to SKIP. A negative value for *count* is invalid.

The usefulness of replicators is that they reduce the size of programs; they do not however introduce new functionality to the language. A replicator can always be expanded (i.e. removed) to produce a longer but equivalent occam program.

3.4.4   IF and CASE

All sequential programming languages require a branch instruction; this usually takes the form of an 'if' statement. In occam the IF constructor is as follows:

```
IF
   b1
      p1
   b2
      p2
   .
   .
   .
   bn
      pn
```

where bj is a Boolean expression and pj is a process. An IF process can contain any number of branches. The termination of the IF is synonymous with the termination of exactly one of the subprocesses. On execution of the IF, b1 is evaluated, if it generates the value TRUE then p1 is executed. If it does not then b2 is evaluated; if this is also FALSE then b3 is tested. Eventually one of the Boolean expressions will generate a TRUE value and the associated subprocess will be executed. This completes the action of the IF. For example, in the following code Y will be set to either -1, 0 or 1 depending on the sign of X:

```
IF
   X < 0
      Y := -1
   X = 0
      Y := 0
   X > 0
      Y := 1
```

The situation in which all the Boolean expressions evaluate to FALSE is deemed to be an error condition. In this circumstance the IF behaves as a STOP. If the logic of one's program implies that on some occasions no action should be taken then this must be stated, explicitly, in the software:

```
IF              -- make X positive
   X < 0
      X := -X
   TRUE         -- always evaluates to true
      SKIP      -- no action
```

However, programmers should resist the temptation to put

```
TRUE
  SKIP
```

at the end of all IF constructs. Only when it is needed should it be used. The following code changes the pattern of lights at a British traffic signal. Boolean variables RED, GREEN and AMBER are used to represent the states of the lights. The channels R, G and A control the lights and the constants OFF and ON give appropriate control signals.

```
IF
  RED AND (NOT AMBER) AND (NOT GREEN)
    SEQ
      A ! ON
      AMBER := TRUE
  RED AND AMBER AND (NOT GREEN)
    SEQ
      R ! OFF
      A ! OFF
      G ! ON
      RED := FALSE
      AMBER := FALSE
      GREEN := TRUE
  GREEN AND (NOT RED) AND (NOT AMBER)
    SEQ
      G ! OFF
      A ! ON
      GREEN := FALSE
      AMBER := TRUE
  AMBER AND (NOT RED) AND (NOT GREEN)
    SEQ
      A ! OFF
      R ! ON
      AMBER := FALSE
      RED := TRUE
```

Note, any other combination of RED, GREEN and AMBER is an incorrect state and the process will STOP. This, in effect, will result in the program terminating. An implementation may support some debugging facilities that will allow the programmer to locate the actual line of the program where the STOP was encountered.

The syntax for the conditional constructor is given by:

```
conditional = IF
                {choice}
```

```
choice =    guarded choice
          | conditional

guarded choice = boolean
                      process
```

This indicates that a branch of an IF constructor can itself be a conditional. The use of this nested structure is described later (Section 3.6.5).

Formally, the semantics of the IF statement can be described as follows. Let the IF process (with n branches) be represented as:

```
 n
 IF biPi
 i = 1
```

where bi is a Boolean expression, and pi is any occam process.
Then

```
 n
 IF biPi = Pj
 i = 1
```

where $NOT(b1)$ AND $NOT(b2)$ AND ... AND $NOT(bj-1)$ AND bj, and

```
 n
 IF biPi = STOP
 i = 1
```

where $NOT(b1)$ AND $NOT(b2)$ AND ... AND $NOT(bn)$.

In these relationships = means equivalent (i.e. the two sides of the relationship have the same effect).

A common form for an IF constructor is a collection of possible actions with the actual one to be chosen being dependent on the value of some variable or simple expression:

```
IF
  I = 1
    P
  I = 2
    Q
  I = 3
    R
```

where P, Q and R are arbitrary processes. Rather than code this structure as an IF process, occam (in common with many other languages) supports a

CASE construct. The use of a CASE process is not only a more logical means of expressing this requirement but it can be implemented much more efficiently. With the occam CASE the above code would be expressed as:

```
CASE I
  1
    P
  2
    Q
  3
    R
```

If, for example, this CASE process is executed with I having the value 3 then R is executed immediately. With the 'equivalent' IF process, first I = 1 is evaluated (to FALSE) then I = 2 (again to FALSE) and finally I = 3 (TRUE) before R is executed.

The general form for the CASE process is defined by:

```
process = CASE selector
              {selection}

selection =    expression
                 process
             | ELSE
                 process

selector = expression
```

On execution of the CASE, selector (which must be of type INT) is evaluated and its value is used to select one of the component selections. If the value of the selector is the same as that of one of the selections then the associated process is executed. The selections are required to have distinct values. In the situation where no selection has the value of the selector then the process following the ELSE is executed. A CASE process can have at most one ELSE part but may have none. If there is no ELSE selection and the value of the selector is such that no actual selection is appropriate (i.e. none has equal value), then the CASE behaves like STOP.

Note that the CASE structure in occam is simpler than that found in most other languages. For example a selection cannot have more than one value or a range.

Replicators can be used with an IF process but this is less common. In the following code an object is read from channel in and is then sent out on one of a number of channels; the one chosen being determined by a local variable V:

```
SEQ
  in ? temp
  -- calculate V
```

```
IF
  V = 1
    OUT[1] ! temp
  V = 2
    OUT[2] ! temp
  V = 3
    OUT[3] ! temp
```

If the code could be constructed in this form, then the following syntax is equivalent but more concise:

```
SEQ
  in ? temp
  -- calculate V
  IF i = 1 FOR 3
    i = V
      OUT[i] ! temp
```

Clearly if a zero replicator is applied the IF becomes equivalent to STOP (if there are no Boolean expressions none of them can evaluate true).

3.5   PAR constructor

So far processes have been introduced but have only been executed sequentially. In order to indicate that two, or more, processes are concurrent the PAR constructor must be used:

```
parallel = PAR
              {process}
```

All subprocesses of a PAR must either be completely independent of each other or interact by using channels and the rendezvous. As an example of the use of PAR, consider the following two element buffer:

```
CHAN OF INT in, out, middle:
PAR
  INT X:
  WHILE TRUE
    SEQ
      in ? X
      middle ! X
  INT X:
  WHILE TRUE
    SEQ
      middle ? X
      out ! X
```

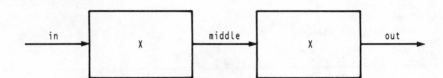

Figure 3.1   A pipeline of two processes.

The program can be usefully represented as a diagram, see Figure 3.1

Within this buffer program two processes are executing concurrently; they interact by use of the channel middle. The buffer would be used, in other parallel processes, by writing to channel in and reading from out.

Both elements of this PAR have a similar form; each consists of a non-terminating loop (acting on a SEQ) and a local variable. The use of a procedure (see Chapter 6) would enable both of these processes to be constructed from a single procedure.

From a program development standpoint PAR has two main uses; firstly, as in the above example, a PAR can be used to express concurrency. This could be in recognition of parallel activities in the application, or to indicate candidates for true parallel execution, or both. An occam program often takes the form of, at the topmost level, a PAR process.

The second use of a PAR is to introduce non-determinacy into the program. This is again a recognition of concurrency but at a lower level, and for a somewhat different reason. In an earlier section an IF process was given for changing the pattern of lights at a traffic signal. Within this IF construct the following sequence was used:

```
SEQ
  R ! OFF
  A ! OFF
  G ! ON
  RED := FALSE
  AMBER := FALSE
  GREEN := TRUE
```

However the computation itself is not a sequential one, and as side-effects cannot be generated in occam the six subprocesses are clearly independent of each other. The SEQ can therefore be replaced by a PAR:

```
PAR
  R ! OFF
  A ! OFF
  G ! ON
  RED := FALSE
  AMBER := FALSE
  GREEN := TRUE
```

The use of PAR in these circumstances has three advantages:

1. It more accurately reflects the properties of the program.
2. It allows the subprocesses to be rearranged and thus enables program transformations to be applied (see Chapter 10).
3. It allows channel operations to be executed in an order determined by the dynamics of the program's execution rather than by a predefined and meaningless sequence.

This last point is the most significant. The assignment processes:

```
RED   := FALSE
AMBER := FALSE
GREEN := TRUE
```

although they are independent, will all terminate immediately (i.e. they cannot lead to suspension) and therefore there is little advantage in explicitly executing them concurrently. Indeed as the implementation of a PAR (see Chapter 8) is more costly than that of a SEQ there are good reasons for not using a PAR. This is not the case with the write operations on the channels:

```
R ! OFF
A ! OFF
G ! ON
```

for it is possible to have a program interleaving in which the processes that are reading from A and G are ready to read but the reader of R is not. With a SEQ constructor all processes will be delayed waiting for this read of R. By comparison, with a PAR constructor the three channel writes will be taken to be concurrent processes and thus the reads on A and G will take place prior to the action on R. (It should perhaps be noted that with a real traffic lights system there are advantages in having all the lights change at the same time.)

This introduction of non-determinacy, in the order in which processes are executed, illustrates that the use of the PAR constructor is not restricted to designating objects for true parallel execution. It is a programming construct that has an important role in all levels of the program.

3.5.1   Termination of a PAR process

As well as indicating that its subprocesses are concurrent, PAR is again a process in its own right. It is therefore appropriate to ask when will it terminate. A PAR process terminates when and only when all of its constituent subprocesses terminate. If the PAR is at the topmost level of an industrial control program then it is common for its subprocesses to have infinite loops within them. They do not terminate, therefore neither does the PAR process nor the program itself.

On the other hand if a PAR process is designed to terminate then the programmer must make sure that all internal processes do also. If only one process remains then the PAR will be prohibited from finishing. A common programming error is to terminate some subprocesses before their neighbours have completed communicating with them. This leaves one process trying to write to (or read from) a channel when the associated process that should read (or write) has terminated. The result is a collection of suspended processes, none of which can become executable again. The run-time system will find that the PAR process cannot terminate but that none of the internal processes are executable. This is a deadlock and the program will fail.

Particular attention should be given to the design of support processes such as buffer or resource controllers. The decision to close down a section of the program must be communicated to all of these agents so that they can themselves terminate and allow the execution of the program to proceed.

3.5.2 PAR replicator

An occam program can be given a concise format if a number of similar processes can be generated, in one go, by the combination of a PAR constructor and a replicator. For example a ten element buffer (see Figure 3.2) can be expressed as:

```
VAL INT N IS 10:
[N + 1]CHAN OF INT C:
PAR
  PAR P = 0 FOR N
    INT BufferElement:
    WHILE TRUE
      SEQ
        C[P] ? BufferElement
        C[P + 1] ! BufferElement
```

The replicator sets up N SEQ processes; by using a one dimensional array of channels the internal communications are catered for. Other processes, that are in parallel with this PAR replicator, could put integers on this buffer by writing to C[0] or extract integers by reading from C[N].

The replicated PAR, like the replicated SEQ, can only be applied to a single subprocess. If it is desirable to act upon a group of processes (SEQ or PAR) then this must be stated explicitly:

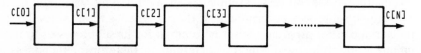

Figure 3.2 A general pipeline of processes.

```
PAR I = 0 FOR N
  PAR
    .
    .
    .
```

For example if p(I) and q(I) are two occam processes whose actions depend upon the value of I then the following code:

```
PAR
  p(1)
  p(2)
  p(3)
  q(1)
  q(2)
  q(3)
```

could be written more concisely as

```
PAR I = 1 FOR 3
  PAR
    p(I)
    q(I)
```

The termination of the replicated PAR is as one would expect (i.e. when all replicated processes have terminated).

As this construction is an important one another example will be given. A parallel equivalent to the usual bubble sort algorithm can be obtained by defining a pipeline of N processes (for N numbers). To sort into increasing order, each process handles two objects (integers in this case) at a time and sends the larger value to its neighbour down the pipeline. It then reads a new value from 'upstream' and repeats the action. The integers are assumed to be positive and the value -1 is used to 'flush' the pipeline:

```
VAL INT FLUSH IS -1:
VAL INT N IS 30:
[N + 1]CHAN OF INT C:
PAR
  -- other processes
  PAR I = 0 FOR N
    INT X,Y:
    SEQ
      C[I] ? X     -- read first value
      WHILE X <> FLUSH
        SEQ
          C[I] ? Y
```

```
        IF
          X > Y
            SEQ
              C[I + 1] ! X
              X := Y
          TRUE
            C[I + 1] ! Y
    C[I + 1] ! FLUSH   -- send on FLUSH value
```

With this code a sequence of up to N integers when written to C[0] (followed by −1) will emerge at C[N] in a sorted order.

3.5.3 Process creation

When a PAR process is executed a number of subprocesses are created. With a replicated PAR the number of processes created is given by the second field of the replicator. In order for the compiler to know how many processes are contained within a program (so that memory allocations and queue length calculations can be undertaken prior to execution) occam does not allow dynamic process creation and thus restricts the second field of a replicator, when used with a PAR, to an expression that can be calculated at compile time. It often takes the form of a constant.

This restriction is, with some applications, significant. Its adverse effect can however be mitigated if the maximum number of possible processes is known at compile time. Consider a PAR replicator that receives its count field value from a channel Start.Value:

```
  -- other processes
  SEQ
    Start.Value ? N
    PAR P = 0 FOR N            -- not valid
      subprocess
```

If the maximum possible value of N is known (MAX) then the following is correct occam and will have only a small run-time overhead even when N is much smaller than MAX:

```
  -- other processes
  INT N:
  VAL INT MAX IS 100:
  SEQ
    Start.Value ? N
    IF
      N <= MAX
        SKIP
    PAR P = 0 FOR MAX        -- valid
```

```
IF
  P <= N
    subprocess
  TRUE
    SKIP
```

The maximum number of processes is always generated but those not required (i.e. when P > N) are only SKIP processes that terminate immediately. As a run-time check, the value of N is compared with MAX, if it is higher the first IF process becomes equivalent to STOP and the process is halted.

3.5.4 Priorities

The PAR constructor enables a number of concurrently executing processes to be generated. How much relative processing time each of these processes gets will depend on the scheduling algorithm employed by the run-time system. It is therefore implementation dependent. In some circumstances it is useful to indicate that some processes are more urgent than others; this can be done by allocating priorities. A high priority process will be given preference over a lower priority one if they are executing on the same processor and the high priority process is executable.

Priorities are allocated in occam by a variant of the PAR constructor called PRI PAR. Each component of a PRI PAR is given a different priority with the textual order being used to indicate a decreasing priority level. A group of processes can be given identical priority by grouping them together within an inner PAR:

```
PRI PAR
  P1                -- highest priority
  PAR
    P2              -- three processes
    P3              -- with middle
    P4              -- priority
  P5                -- lowest priority
```

With a normal computation the dependence between the processes means that the use of a PRI PAR does not have a significant effect upon system performance. If some processes are allocated more processor time then others will, inevitably, have less and the complete system will behave much as before. Where the PRI PAR is useful is in real-time systems where it is necessary to respond quickly to some external event. By allocating the highest priority to the process that must handle the response, the programmer will ensure that other processes will not be executed until the real-time event is handled.

As the run-time system must support distinct queues for each priority level an implementation may limit the number of components that can be contained in a PRI PAR. For example, on the transputer only two priority levels are supported.

3.5.5   PLACED PAR

Once a program has been designed, developed and verified its final execution may be assigned to a number of processors. Another variant of the PAR constructor is used for this purpose. The PLACED PAR indicates that the associated subprocesses are not only concurrent but they are to be allocated to different processors and will therefore be truly parallel:

```
parallel =   PLACED PAR
               {placement}
           | PLACED PAR replicator
             placement

placement = PROCESSOR expression
             process
```

for example:

```
PLACED PAR
  PROCESSOR 1
    P1
  PROCESSOR 2
    P2
```

Where P1 and P2 are processes (possibly PAR or PRI PAR) and the numbers 1 and 2 are implementation dependent (expressions). A replicator may also be applied to a PLACED PAR. Each of the available processors is assumed to have a unique integer value. This mapping of processes to processors is considered in more detail in Chapter 8.

3.6   ALT constructor

The PAR constructor allows for non-determinacy by enabling a collection of subprocesses to be executed in whatever order is appropriate for that particular execution of the program. It was mentioned in the previous chapter that another form of non-determinacy is needed with message based languages; this enables a process to choose between a number of possible sources of message. Figure 3.3 illustrates a simple concentrator process.

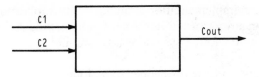

Figure 3.3   A merge process.

Two sequences of objects, arriving down channels C1 and C2, are to be merged into a single Cout channel. With the constructors that have so far been described this cannot be achieved in a flexible way. The ALT constructor provides the necessary structure:

```
INT X:
WHILE TRUE
  ALT
    C1 ? X        -- alternative 1
      Cout ! X
    C2 ? X        -- alternative 2
      Cout ! X
```

For each execution of the ALT, one (and only one) of the alternatives is selected. The general form of the ALT is

```
ALT
  G1
    P1
  G2
    P2
  .
  .
  .
  Gn
    Pn
```

Where G_i is a guard and P_i is a subprocess. The simplest form for a guard is an input process; if there is an object waiting to be input (i.e. there is another process committed to writing to this ALT process) then the guard is said to be **ready**. The execution of the ALT process involves picking a ready guard, executing the input process of the guard and then executing the associated subprocess. This subprocess can be arbitrarily complex. If there is no ready guard then the ALT process will be suspended until there is one. By contrast, if there is more than one ready guard then an arbitrary choice is made between these ready guards.

Arbitrary here means that the language definition does not specify which algorithm an implementation should use. By implication a program should not rely on any particular implementation method as the movement of the program on to another system could result in the program behaving incorrectly.

The alternative constructor is defined as follows:

```
alternation = ALT
                {alternative}

alternative =   guarded alternative
              | alternation

guarded alternative = guard
                           process
```

3.6.1   Guards

Guards are used to avoid specific communications during the execution of the ALT constructor. This is the main method of providing condition synchronization in occam. The occam guard can take one of a number of forms:

```
guard =   input
        | Boolean & input
        | Boolean & SKIP
```

For example:

```
chan ? X            -- input guard

A > B & chan ? X    -- Boolean expression and input guard

A < B & SKIP        -- effectively Boolean expression only

Time ? AFTER T      -- timeout, Time being a TIMER
```

The guard is ready when the Boolean expression evaluates to TRUE and the associated process can execute. With a SKIP this is immediate; with an input process this is when there is an object to read (i.e. some other process is waiting to output to that channel). Care should be taken when using the SKIP form of the guard; if the associated Boolean expression (which must be present but could be simply TRUE) evaluates TRUE then that alternative could always be taken even when there are outstanding ready input guards. Moreover if the ALT constructor is placed within a loop (as is common) the existence of a permanently ready SKIP alternative can lead to polling which is wasteful of processor time.

With the timeout form, the guard is ready when the timeout expires, i.e. when the value of the local clock is greater than the expression T. As its name implies it is used to program situations where it is necessary to recognize (and deal with) the non-appearance of data down a channel (or collection of channels). For example the following code will wait a thousand units of time for an input from channel ch. If no rendezvous takes place within that time the program executes some error recovery procedure:

```
TIMER Clock:
SEQ
  Clock ? time
  ALT
    ch ? Some.Variable
      -- normal action
    Clock ? AFTER time PLUS 1000
      -- error recovery action
```

In this code the operator PLUS is used (rather than +) because it gives a modulus result which is necessary with time expressions – see the next chapter. The action of a timeout can be inhibited by combining it with a Boolean expression in the guard:

```
Timeout.On & Time ? AFTER T
```

3.6.2 Circular buffer

To illustrate the use of ALT processes (with guards) a simple buffer agent will be considered. Buffers are a useful concurrent programming tool. They allow active processes in a pipeline to decouple their execution by communicating via a buffer rather than directly. A common form for such buffers is a circular or bounded buffer. The buffer is represented as a vector (of appropriate data type) with two pointers. One pointer indicates the next free slot on the buffer; the other points to the next object to be taken from the buffer (see Figure 3.4).

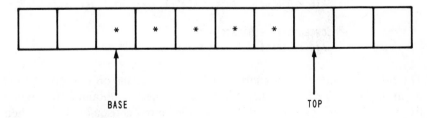

Figure 3.4   A FIFO buffer.

With each PUT or GET operation on the buffer the associated pointers are incremented; by using modular arithmetic the pointers wrap around the top of the vector; hence the term circular buffer.

In order to code a circular buffer reliably in a concurrent programming language two condition synchronizations must be implemented; it must not be possible to GET from an empty buffer or PUT on to a full one.

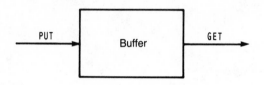

Figure 3.5   A buffer process.

An occam buffer process (see Figure 3.5) should have an interface of two channels (GET and PUT); however the following code which deals with GET and PUT symmetrically (and is the natural way one would expect to structure the code) is not correct:

```
CHAN OF INT PUT, GET:
PAR
  VAL INT Buf.Size IS 32:
  INT TOP, BASE, CONTENTS:
  [Buf.Size]INT BUFFER:
  SEQ
    CONTENTS := 0
    TOP := 0
    BASE := 0
    WHILE TRUE
      ALT
        CONTENTS < Buf.Size & PUT ? BUFFER [TOP]
          SEQ
            CONTENTS := CONTENTS + 1
            TOP := (TOP + 1) REM Buf.Size
        CONTENTS > 0 & GET ! Buffer [BASE]   -- not legal occam
          SEQ
            CONTENTS := CONTENTS - 1
            BASE := (BASE + 1) REM Buf.Size
```

The first alternative has a guard which evaluates TRUE only when there is room in the buffer for another object. This object is obtained by reading from channel PUT. If such an input is possible, and is chosen by the ALT, then the CONTENTS and TOP variables are incremented.

The problem with this code is that it contains an output operation in the guard of the second alternative. This is not allowed in occam due to the semantic difficulties that arise if both input and output operations on a single channel are contained in guards in different ALT processes. If this were the case then the choice of an alternative in one ALT process would have to depend on the choice made in the other (and vice versa). This would cause significant implementation difficulties particularly if the two ALT processes were contained on different processors (Andrews and Schneider, 1983; Buckley and Silberschatz, 1983; Francez Yemini, 1985).

A correct occam implementation of a circular buffer is obtained by introducing another process and inverting the GET communication with the buffer (see Figure 3.6):

```
CHAN OF INT PUT, GET, Request, Reply:
PAR
  VAL INT Buf.Size IS 32:
  INT TOP, BASE, CONTENTS:
  [Buf.Size]INT BUFFER:
  SEQ
    CONTENTS := 0
    TOP := 0
    BASE := 0
    INT Any:
    WHILE TRUE
      ALT
        CONTENTS < Buf.Size & PUT ? BUFFER [TOP]
          SEQ
            CONTENTS := CONTENTS + 1
            TOP := (TOP + 1) REM Buf.Size
        CONTENTS > 0 & Request ? Any
          SEQ
            Reply ! BUFFER[BASE]
            CONTENTS := CONTENTS - 1
            BASE := (BASE + 1) REM Buf.Size
  INT Temp:    -- single buffer process
  VAL INT Any IS 0:    -- dummy value
  WHILE TRUE
    SEQ
      Request ! Any
      Reply ? Temp
      GET ! Temp
```

This is, in effect, a Buf.Size + 1 buffer as one element will be contained in the single buffer process. To read from the buffer, the single element process first indicates that it wishes to read (by synchronizing down channel Request) and then actually reads via channel Reply. The client process is however unaffected as it still obtains data via the GET channel.

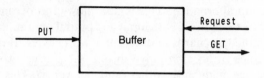

Figure 3.6   A programmable buffer process.

In the above occam program the interaction between the main buffer and the single buffer process takes the form of a double rendezvous. This is a common structure in occam programs; a process sends a request via one channel and receives the reply on another:

```
        Client                          Server
     request ! data                  request ? input
     reply ? results                       .
                                           .
                                           .
                               reply ! output
```

With the server process it may be necessary to wait for resources to be released before the reply value can be sent.

Request/reply message couples in this form can be reliably coded in occam because the client cannot 'disappear' between making the request and receiving the reply. If occam provided an abort statement (whereby one process can abort another) then the production of reliable algorithms would be much more difficult. For instance if the client above was aborted between the two rendezvous then the server would be deadlocked.

3.6.3   A proportional controller

In order to give another illustration of the use of the ALT constructor a simple proportional controller will be considered (see Figure 3.7). Such a controller reads input data and compares it with a desired value for that data. If the two are not identical a new output signal is generated.

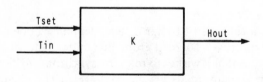

Figure 3.7   A controller process.

The output value Hout is obtained from the input value Tin by the formula:

```
Hout := K(Tset - Tin)
```

where K is known as the proportional gain and Tset is the desired value of Tin. For example T could be a temperature reading and Hout a heater setting. If the input value is lower than that required the heater is turned up; alternatively if the temperature is too high the heater is given a signal that will turn it down. The code for such a controller could have the following form (the definitions of the variables used are omitted for clarity):

```
SEQ
  SET.VALUE ? Tset  -- read a Tset value to start with
  WHILE TRUE
    ALT
      SET.VALUE ? Tset
        SKIP
      Treading ? Tin
        H.VALUE ! K*(Tset - Tin)
```

Initially a value for Tset must be read from channel SET.VALUE; after this has been obtained the controller process loops round either reading a new value for Tset (in which case it does nothing more than take note of the new value) or reading a value of Tin and then outputting a new Hout value down channel H.VALUE.

With many controllers it is necessary to take remedial action if the controlled device goes off-line. In the above code this would be signified by a lack of values coming down Treading. A proportional controller with timeout is illustrated in Figure 3.8.

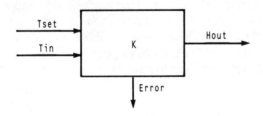

Figure 3.8   A controller process with error output.

The occam code is as follows:

```
TIMER clock:
VAL INT Any IS 0:   -- dummy value
SEQ
  clock ? Time
  SET.VALUE ? Tset
  WHILE TRUE
```

```
ALT
    SET.VALUE ? Tset
      SKIP
    Treading ? Tin
      SEQ
         clock ? Time
         H.VALUE ! K*(Tset - Tin)
    clock ? AFTER Time PLUS TimeOut
      SEQ
         clock ? Time
         Error.Channel ! Any
```

Here the ALT process has three alternatives. The first merely gets a new value of Tset, the second (which will be the normal action) reads a new Tin value, outputs a new value down H.VALUE and resets the timeout by reading from the clock. Although these two actions are independent they are executed in a SEQ because the clock input cannot lead to delay and hence there would be no advantage in using a PAR. The third alternative in the ALT is the timeout; the guard clock? AFTER Time PLUS Timeout becomes ready when the value on the TIMER is greater than Time PLUS Timeout. If this happens before either of the other two guards becomes ready then the third alternative will be taken. This will result in a synchronization down the error channel and a new value of Time being obtained. If no further data appears down Treading then the controller will synchronize down Error.Channel at regular intervals (i.e. every Timeout).

Note that although the reading of a new value for Tset will terminate that execution of the ALT (and thereby cancel the timeout even though no value has appeared down Treading) the next time the ALT is executed the timeout period will be shorter. For example if the timeout was 5 seconds and after 2 seconds a communication down SET.VALUE took place then when the ALT is executed again the timeout value would be only 3 seconds (approximately).

A further refinement to the above program would be to add a 'user interface' which could be used to enquire what the present Tin value is:

```
TIMER clock:
INT Any:
SEQ
  clock ? Time
  SET.VALUE ? Tset
  WHILE TRUE
    ALT
      SET.VALUE ? Tset
        SKIP
      Treading ? Tin
        SEQ
           clock ? Time
           H.VALUE ! K*(Tset - Tin)
```

```
    clock ? AFTER Time PLUS TimeOut
      SEQ
        clock ? Time
        Error.Channel ! Any
    Enquire ? Any
      UserOutput ! Tin
```

Finally high and low alarm levels can be set so that if Tin is ever out of range a warning is given. This warning would take the form of synchronizations down appropriate channels:

```
TIMER clock:
INT Any:
SEQ
  clock ? Time
  SET.VALUE ? Tset
  WHILE TRUE
    ALT
      SET.VALUE ? Tset
        SKIP
      Treading ? Tin
        PAR
          clock ? Time
          H.VALUE ! K*(Tset − Tin)
          IF
            Tin > HIGH
              High.Level ! Any
            Tin < LOW
              Low.Level ! Any
            TRUE
              SKIP
      clock ? AFTER Time PLUS TimeOut
        SEQ
          clock ? Time
          Error.Channel ! Any
      Enquire ? Any
        UserOutput ! Tin
```

3.6.4   Asynchronous communication

In the above examples of simple controller processes it is important that the controllers themselves are always responsive to the inputs that are being serviced. One means of obtaining this responsiveness is to run the controller process at a high priority (using PRI PAR). However as a result of the synchronous communication which is implicit in the rendezvous it is possible for the controller to be blocked on any of its output operations. For example the communication of a new Hout value down channel H.VALUE will lead to the controller being suspended until the process that reads from that channel is in a position to do so. If this read process is tardy then the controller will remain suspended and will not be able to respond to a new, possibly dangerous, reading of Tin.

To program asynchronous communication requires the introduction of a buffer process. This concurrent process will take values from the controller and make the most recent available to the reading (or client) process. Both of these actions are synchronized but the overall effect is to free the controller from waiting for the client process; it merely waits for the responsive buffer. To illustrate the use of a buffer process consider the control output given in the process above:

```
H.VALUE ! K*(Tset — Tin)
```

The process that is acting as the device driver for the output device will rendezvous (synchronously) with the controller using the same channel:

```
H.VALUE ? New.Setting
```

By introducing two new channels Buffer.Get and Buffer.Out, and reversing the communication with the device driver (as was done with the circular buffer), the buffer process can be constructed as follows:

```
INT Buffer.Value:
SEQ
  H.VALUE ? Buffer.Value
  INT Any:
  WHILE TRUE
    ALT
      H.VALUE ? Buffer.Value
        SKIP
      Buffer.Get ? Any
        Buffer.Out ! Buffer.Value
```

Note that initially a value is read from H.VALUE into the buffer variable.

The client process, when it is in a position to read a new setting, synchronizes down channel Buffer.Get and then reads from Buffer.Out:

```
VAL Any IS 0:
SEQ
  Buffer.Get ! Any
  Buffer.Out ? New.Setting
```

As a consequence of this structure the client process will always get an up to date value of Hout although it need not read every value generated by the controller. It could however loop round continuously reading a value that does not change; to remove this possible busy loop a guard could be used in the buffer to stop the ALT choosing to communicate on channel Buffer.Get unless a new value was available:

```
BOOL New.Value:  -- set to TRUE if a new value available
INT Buffer.Value:
SEQ
  H.VALUE ? Buffer.Value
  New.Value := TRUE
  INT Any:
  WHILE TRUE
    ALT
      H.VALUE ? Buffer.Value
        New.Value := TRUE
      New.Value & Buffer.Get ? Any
        SEQ
          Buffer.Out ! Buffer.Value
          New.Value := FALSE
```

Care must however be taken with this structure to protect the client process from being blocked if no new value is ever generated.

3.6.5 ALT replicator

The ALT constructor is often used to multiplex a number of input channels on to one output channel or to code a server process that is receiving requests via a number of input channels. If the input channels can be represented as elements of a vector of channels, then a replicated ALT can be used to give a concise syntactical form:

```
VAL INT Max IS 32:
[Max]CHAN OF INT Request:
PAR
  WHILE TRUE
    ALT I = 0 FOR Max
      Request[I] ? temp
        -- some action
```

This is equivalent to the expanded form one obtains if the replicator is removed:

```
VAL INT Max IS 32:
[Max]CHAN OF INT Request:
PAR
  WHILE TRUE
    ALT
      Request[0] ? temp
        -- some action
```

```
Request[1] ? temp
  -- same action
Request[2] ? temp
  -- same action
Request[3] ? temp
  -- same action
      .
      .
      .

Request[31] ? temp
  -- same action
```

Care must be taken to make sure the ALT replicator has at least one replication, otherwise the ALT will have no alternatives and is thus equivalent to STOP.

Although the symmetric naming structure used in occam makes it impossible to write general purpose server processes (because the number of clients must be known beforehand) the use of a replicator with an ALT does enable code that is only dependent upon a single constant to be re-used.

In some circumstances (for example those illustrated in Figure 3.9) an ALT process may wish to choose between a single channel or one of a vector.

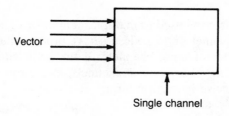

Vector

Single channel

Figure 3.9   Merging a single channel with a vector of channels.

The vector can be accommodated with a replicator but this cannot also handle the other single channel. To deal with this situation occam allows one of the alternatives within an ALT constructor itself to be an ALT constructor (see definition of alternation above):

```
ALT
  ALT I = 1 FOR Max
    Request[I] ? t1
      -- some action
    SingleChannel ? t2
      -- some other action
```

All the alternatives, nested or otherwise, are given equal significance within the outer ALT.

This facility for allowing ALT constructors to be nested also applies to the IF constructor.

3.6.6 PRI ALT

We have already seen that if an ALT process has more than one ready guard then the one chosen for execution is not defined in the language. This enables an implementation to optimize how it executes the ALT construct. Nevertheless, in a number of situations it is necessary to give preference to certain communications. This can be achieved by using appropriate Boolean expressions in the guards, but the code becomes inelegant. To remove the need for such expressions occam provides a variant of the ALT constructor which has a non-arbitrary algorithm:

```
PRI ALT
  G1
    P1
  G2
    P2
  .
  .
  .
  Gn
    Pn
```

The PRI ALT process behaves identically to the normal ALT except in the situation where there is more than one ready guard. In this event the ready guard that is textually first is the one that is chosen. For example in the proportion controller illustrated above it may be desirable to give priority to a communication that is changing the set point:

```
WHILE TRUE
  PRI ALT
    SET.VALUE ? Tset
      SKIP
    Treading ? Tin
      H.VALUE ! K * (Tset — Tin)
```

Similarly in the asynchronous buffer example priority should be given to the H.VALUE read so that the controller is not blocked unnecessarily:

```
BOOL New.Value:  —— set to TRUE if a new value available
INT Buffer.Value:
SEQ
  H.VALUE ? Buffer.Value
  New.Value := TRUE
  INT Any:
  WHILE TRUE
```

```
PRI ALT
  H.VALUE ? Buffer.Value
    New.Value := TRUE
  New.Value & Buffer.Get ? Any
    SEQ
      Buffer.Out ! Buffer.Value
      New.Value := FALSE
```

As the algorithm used to implement a normal ALT is arbitrary, an implementation could use this textual order for both PRI ALT and ALT. A programmer should have, however, a clear view as to the distinction between the two. In particular it should be possible to rearrange the alternatives within an ALT construct without significantly affecting the behaviour of the program. The program should be invariant to the ordering within ALT constructors. If this is not the case then there are liveness problems that should be addressed directly. A PRI ALT can be integrated within a nested ALT to implement algorithms such as:

```
WHILE TRUE
  PRI ALT
    SingleChannel ? t2
      SKIP
    ALT I = 1 FOR SIZE
      Requested[I] ? t1
        Return ! t1 * t2
```

This code reads from a vector of channels, multiplies the readings by a factor t2 and outputs the new value down channel Return. Preference is given to a communication down SingleChannel as this is used to change the value of t2.

There is one situation in which the behaviour of PRI ALT does not take account of the textual order of the ready guards. This is when the PRI ALT is first executed with no ready guards (i.e. it is suspended) and then two guards become ready simultaneously. In this case either of the guards is chosen; the textual order is not significant. For example consider the following code:

```
PRI ALT
  A > 0 & ch ? X
    -- action
  B > 0 & ch ? Y
    -- different action
```

Firstly, it should be noted that this is correct code for a PRI ALT or ALT constructor. It is quite acceptable to have the same channel mentioned in more than one guard; although the associated Boolean expressions would usually preclude the possibility of both guards being ready simultaneously. However with the above code if A and B are both greater than zero then, if there is already a process waiting to output to ch, the execution of the PRI ALT will favour the first guard. If, on the other hand, the PRI ALT process is suspended when the output request on ch is made then the semantics of the PRI ALT do not guarantee that the second guard will not be picked for execution. This seemingly peculiar distinction makes implementation of the PRI ALT easier.

The above code interestingly illustrates another property of the ALT constructor; what would happen if A and B were both less than zero? Clearly neither of the guards can ever be ready. The ALT is thus equivalent to the primitive process STOP. Care should be taken to ensure that all the Boolean expressions (within guards) are related in such a way as for it to be impossible for them all to be FALSE. Of course the guard:

```
ch ? X
```

is equivalent to:

```
TRUE & ch ? X
```

and ensures that the ALT process does not suffer from this difficulty.

It was mentioned earlier in this section that a guard of the form TRUE & SKIP effectively reduces an ALT statement, which contains it, to a simple process. This is because the guard is always ready and can therefore always be chosen. Where this guard can be useful, however, is as the last alternative in a PRI ALT. Consider, for illustration, a process that loops round outputting down channel out a series of increasing integers:

```
SEQ
  n := 0
  WHILE TRUE
    SEQ
      out ! n
      n := n + 1
```

Periodically this process receives a communication, through channel in, which resets the integer n. It is necessary therefore to check for the existence of a new input each time the process loops. However the process does not wish to wait for a new value if there is not one immediately available. To achieve this behaviour the process must be changed to include a PRI ALT:

```
SEQ
  n := 0
  WHILE TRUE
```

```
PRI ALT
  in ? n
    SKIP
  TRUE & SKIP
    SEQ
      out ! n
      n := n + 1
```

The PRI ALT is needed so that the input is guaranteed to be taken if a communication is possible.

This use of a TRUE & SKIP guard in a PRI ALT, although illustrated only by a simple example above, is an important construct with many uses. Care must however be taken to ensure that busy wait loops are not programmed. A busy wait loop is one in which a process continually executes without becoming suspended but without performing any worthwhile computations. This can constitute a livelock.

3.7   Rules of association

In this chapter most of the program structures of occam have been described; primitive processes, blocks and the SEQ, PAR, IF, CASE, WHILE and ALT constructors have all been considered. The only significant language structure remaining is the PROC (see Chapter 6). However before going on to describe data types, in the next chapter, an important property of the PAR and SEQ constructors is analysed. Both of these constructs obey the rule of association; for example the following two programs are equivalent:

```
SEQ                SEQ
  SEQ                A
    A                SEQ
    B                  B
  C                    C
```

where A, B and C are processes. Indeed both of the above programs are equivalent to:

```
SEQ
  A
  B
  C
```

That is, a sequence of sequences is itself a sequence.

An identical rule also applied to PAR. Although this property of association is in many ways obvious it is the first example we have met, in this book, of a transformation to a program that is guaranteed not to affect the meaning of the program. The topic of transformations is an important one in occam and is considered at length in Chapter 10.

Before concluding this chapter, however, two further simple transformations will be given. Because the components of a PAR are concurrent it is possible to rearrange these components into whatever order is required:

```
PAR              PAR              PAR
  A                C                B
  B                B                A
  C                A                C
```

Finally, and most importantly, occam allows a SEQ to be replaced by a PAR if the components of the SEQ are independent of one another:

```
SEQ        →      PAR
  A                A
  B                B
```

where A and B have no shared variables or channels in common. This transformation is correct, as the evaluation of an expression cannot have side-effects even if it involves a function call. If syntactically two processes are unrelated then their executions will also be independent. This is, of course, not the case with languages that have functions that can act on non-local data.

The motivation for this final transformation is to increase the parallelism within the program. Even though the execution of a PAR process is more expensive than that of a SEQ (see Chapter 8) the increased non-determinism is usually of benefit. The use of the above transformations is illustrated by the following example:

```
SEQ
  in1 ? X
  Y := Y + X        -- for some Y
  in2 ? P
  P := P + Y
```

A value is read down channel in1 added to Y, which is then added to P (the initial value of P being read from channel in2).

By the rule of association this is equivalent to:

```
SEQ
  SEQ
    in1 ? X
    Y := Y + X
    in2 ? P
  P := P + Y
```

And again:

```
SEQ
  SEQ       -- SEQ with two independent components
    SEQ
      in1 ? X
      Y := Y + X
    in2 ? P
  P := P + Y
```

The labelled SEQ can now be replaced by a PAR:

```
SEQ
  PAR
    SEQ
      in1 ? X
      Y := Y + X
    in2 ? P
  P := P + Y
```

The two channel operations are now concurrent; the program being transformed by the repeated application of simple rules. As indicated above this topic is discussed in detail in Chapter 10.

CHAPTER 4

Data Types

Most books that examine programming languages give equal coverage to the control structures and data types supported by the language. In introducing occam more attention has been given here to the control structures. This is because they represent the novel and powerful features of the language. Nevertheless without a model for representing data the language would clearly be incomplete. This chapter considers this data model.

Although user defined scalar types cannot be used in occam there are available a number of predefined data types:

- INT – an integer type; defined to be the one that an implementation can best support (this will be a multiple of 8 bits in length).
- BYTE – integer type with range 0 ... 255.
- BOOL – Boolean type with values TRUE and FALSE.

An implementation may also support explicit 16, 32 and 64-bit integers (INT16, INT32 and INT64).

These simple types, together with CHAN and TIMER, are known as **primitive types**.

Hexadecimal integer constants are allowed; these are designated by a preceding #. Byte constants can be represented by characters; they are defined within single quotes and have the value given by the associated ASCII code. The character * can be used to gain access to the non-printable characters:

```
'a'    -- ascii a, internal representation 97
'C'    -- ascii C
'*c'   -- carriage return
'*n'   -- newline
'**'   -- ascii *
'*''   -- ascii '
```

In addition to the above integer based types there are two floating point representations:

- REAL32 – 32-bit real defined by ANSI/IEEE standard 754-1985,
- REAL64 – 64-bit real defined by ANSI/IEEE standard 754-1985.

By giving a strict definition to floating point values a computation undertaken on a host system should generate the same results as one executed on the target. Some implementations of occam, though not that on the transputer, may however also provide a type REAL which will be defined, like INT, to be the one that an implementation can best support. This will be needed as many 32-bit machines have a floating point representation that is different from the ANSI/IEEE standard. Real numbers must contain a '.', and may be raised to a power of ten by the exponential operator E. A detailed description of the representation of reals is given in Appendix C.

The full range of primitive types is given by:

```
primitive type =   CHAN OF P
               |   TIMER
               |   BOOL
               |   BYTE
               |   INT
               |   REAL32
               |   REAL64
               |   REAL
               |   INT16
               |   INT32
               |   INT64
```

The range of types available in occam is defined by;

```
type =   primitive type
     |   PORT OF type
     |   array type
     |   record type
```

The primitive type PORT is considered later (Chapter 9).

Variables are declared to be of a particular type by listing them after the name of the type:

```
INT I, J, K:
INT16 L:
BOOL Stop, Go, Action:
BYTE Char:
REAL32 X, Y, Z:
```

The list is terminated by a colon.

All variables must of course be defined and are associated with a single type. All primitive types (apart from CHAN and TIMER) have the assignment operator defined. Literals can also be used with all these data types. Some examples of the use of literals are:

```
I := 4
L := 42
Stop := FALSE
Char := 'q'
X := 6.42
Y := 0.7E+3        -- 700.0
Z := 1.0E-3        -- 0.001
```

Real literals are rounded if they do not have an exact representation in that type. In order to clarify the type of a literal a type tag, in parentheses, may be added, for example:

```
X := 6.42(REAL32)
L := 42(INT16)
```

This mechanism can also be used to give a limited form of retyping; i.e. a character literal (which is of type BYTE) can be interpreted as a value of another integer type;

```
J := 'A'(INT)
```

Named constants are defined by abbreviations (see Chapter 6):

```
VAL INT MAX IS 1024:
VAL REAL32 PI IS 3.1415926:
```

These declare an INT constant called MAX with a value 1024 and a REAL32 constant PI with an appropriate value.

For all integer types occam provides two operators for finding the most negative and most positive values which variables of that type can take. These operators are called MOSTPOS and MOSTNEG.

4.1 Expressions

The usual arithmetic operations are available for integers and reals:

```
I + J      -- addition
X - Y      -- subtraction
```

```
I * J    -- multiplication
Y / Z    -- division of reals
I / J    -- division of integers (round down)
I \ J    -- remainder operation
```

If during the evaluation of these expressions an overflow condition occurs then the associated process is deemed to have executed a STOP. The operators PLUS, MINUS and TIMES can, however, be used to wrap round (i.e. they are modulo operators). Thus MOSTPOS PLUS 1 is equal to MOSTNEG; whereas MOSTPOS + 1 will cause STOP. These variants are particularly useful when dealing with real-time as the values given by a TIMER do themselves wrap round. The following delay is therefore coded reliably even when the clock resets itself:

```
VAL INT DELAY IS  5000:
INT T:
TIMER Clock:
SEQ
  Clock ? T
  Clock ? AFTER T PLUS DELAY
```

Indeed the TIMER itself executes a PLUS 1 operation for each increment of the clock value.

Within occam each type has an implicit order and therefore the relational operators can be applied to all variables (of the same type):

```
I = J     -- equal
I > J     -- greater than
I < J     -- less than
I >= J    -- greater than or equal
I <= J    -- less than or equal
I <> J    -- not equal
```

Boolean variables have the NOT, AND and OR operators defined:

```
Go OR Action
Stop AND NOT Action
```

In addition to these operators that one would expect to see in a high level language, there are six that view an INT (or BYTE) as a string of distinct bits:

```
I /\ J    -- bitwise AND
I \/ J    -- bitwise OR
~ J       -- bitwise NOT
I >< J    -- bitwise Exclusive OR
I >> 3    -- shift I to the right by three places
I << 4    -- shift I to the left by four places
```

The shift operators both fill with zeros.

If an implementation does not provide the symbols \ and ˜ then the affected operators may be known as REM (\), BITAND (/\), BITOR (\/) and BITNOT (˜).

An expression is defined to be an operand followed by an operator followed by another operand (there are also unary operators, for example NOT and -). The operand itself can be either a variable name, a constant or an expression. However if the operand is an expression it MUST be contained in brackets. Therefore X + Y + Z will not compile, it must be expressed as either X + (Y + Z) or (X + Y) + Z. As a consequence of this rule there is no requirement to define operator precedence.

4.2   The type model

Implicit within the concept of data typing is the idea that an expression should contain only objects of the same type. There should be no implicit type changes. If it is desirable to mix types within an expression then this must be represented explicitly by using a type conversion. All types are assumed to be built from the same base and therefore conversions are allowed between all objects. A type conversion has one of three forms:

```
conversion =   type operand
           |   type ROUND operand
           |   type TRUNC operand
```

For instance:

```
z := T e
z := T ROUND e
z := T TRUNC e
```

where z is of type T and e is an expression in another primitive type. The effect of these conversions is to obtain a value of type T that is a representation of, or approximation for, the value of e.

If the two primitive types have the same underlying structure, so that values have identical representation in both types, then the conversion can be expressed exactly.

```
INT I:
BYTE B:
SEQ
  B := 'X'   -- ascii code
  I := INT B
```

If during execution a conversion would give rise to an invalid representation, for example

```
SEQ
  I := 5012
  B := BYTE I
```

then the conversion becomes equivalent to STOP.

When the two types have different representations then a rounding or truncation preference must be stated. In particular conversions between integers and reals must take one of these forms:

```
INT I,J,K:
REAL32 X,Y:
SEQ
  I := 7
  X := 7.7777
  J := INT TRUNC X    -- J has value 7
  K := INT ROUND X    -- K has value 8
  Y := REAL32 ROUND I
```

The use of retyping to allow a representation to be interpreted as a variable of another type is considered in Chapter 6.

4.3 Arrays

The main structured data type in occam is the array:

```
array type = [expression]type
```

For example:

```
[32]INT X,Y,Z:
[16]REAL32 A,B,C:
```

The constants contained in square brackets gives the size of the array; indexing is from zero. Every array must contain at least one component. Each element in the array can be accessed by means of a subscript:

```
SEQ I = 0 FOR 32
  ch ? X[I]
```

A run-time check on array bounds violation is undertaken on most implementations. As always an invalid state is synonymous with the STOP process.

Multidimensional arrays are constructed as arrays of arrays:

```
[16][32]INT MAT:
SEQ
  SEQ I = 0 FOR 16
    SEQ J = 0 FOR 32
      ch ? MAT[I][J]
```

This defines an array with 16 elements, each element of which is itself a 32-element array. To read, or write, to an element of this structure therefore requires two subscripts; the first being within the range 0...15, the second within 0...31. The two replicated SEQs (in the above code) cause I and J to loop through all allowable values for these subscripts and hence the complete array is filled with integer values coming down channel ch (i.e. first MAT[0][0] is given a value, then MAT[0][1], then MAT[0][2], ..., MAT[0][31], MAT[1][0], MAT[1][1], ..., MAT[15][31]).

Any number of dimensions can be supported (available memory being the ultimate restriction); and any type can be used. Multidimensional arrays of channels are also allowed.

Apart from the restriction that the lower bound on all dimensions must be zero, occam arrays have no special characteristics. To support the production of general purpose code, constants can be used:

```
VAL INT Depth IS 16:
VAL INT Width IS 32:
[Depth][Width]INT MAT:
SEQ
  SEQ I = 0 FOR Depth
    SEQ J = 0 FOR Width
      ch ? MAT[I][J]
```

Alternatively the size of any dimension of any array can be obtained by using the operator SIZE:

```
SEQ I = 0 FOR SIZE X
  ch ? X[I]

SEQ
  SEQ I = 0 FOR SIZE MAT
    SEQ J = 0 FOR SIZE MAT [0]
      ch ! MAT[I][J]
```

In the first example X is any one dimensional array. The replicated SEQ therefore loops through the entire array. The second example is the two dimensional array illustrated earlier; the value of 16 is obtained by taking the SIZE of MAT, 32 comes from applying SIZE to any element of MAT.

Two arrays are considered to have the same type if they have the same number of components and these components are of the same type. Whole array assignments are available between structures of the same type:

```
[32][16]INT MAT:
[16]INT A,B:
[16]INT C:
SEQ
  -- generate A
  B := A
  C := B
  SEQ I = 0 FOR SIZE [0]MAT
    MAT[I] := A
```

In the last part of this example each element of the first dimension of MAT is assigned the value A. This is appropriate as each side of the assignment is a 16-element INT array.

Assignments between arrays can be implemented more effectively than a series of simple element operations, although in the above example the assignment of A to B is functionally equivalent to:

```
SEQ I = 0 FOR 16
  B[I] := A[I]
```

As well as complete array assignments the communication of complete arrays down channels is supported in occam:

```
ch ! A
ch ? B
```

However for this to be syntactically correct the protocol for the channel ch has to be correctly defined. This is dealt with in the next chapter.

4.3.1 Array constants

Array literals are expressed as a series of data literals separated by commas and contained within square brackets. For example consider a short integer array that is to be given a set of initial values:

```
[4]INT Fred:
SEQ
  Fred := [1,2,4,8]
```

To be valid the array literal must contain the same number of components as there are elements in the array.

A two (or more) dimensional array can similarly be assigned values:

```
[3][2]INT Dbt:
SEQ
  Dbt := [[7,11],[2,5],[4,3]]
```

Here the value of, say, Dbt[2][1] after the assignment is 3.

Another example of an array constant is the following which involves an array of BYTE:

```
[6]BYTE Grades:
SEQ
  Grades := ['A','B','C','D','E','F']
```

4.3.2 Strings

Constant arrays of bytes can also be represented as strings. A string is a series of ASCII characters bracketed by quotation marks:

```
"ABCD"
"Frank Zappa"
```

A string can be assigned to a BYTE array provided that the number of elements is the same:

```
Grades := "ABCDEF"
```

The length of a string can be obtained by using the SIZE operator; for example the following process outputs all the Grades down channel out:

```
SEQ I = 0 FOR SIZE Grades
  out ! Grades[I]
```

An alternative approach is to store the length of the string in its first byte. The compiler can be forced to do this by placing the character *1 immediately after the first "; the value of byte 0 is then the subscript of the last character of the string:

```
Grades := "*1ABCDEF"
SEQ I = 1 FOR Grades[0]
  out ! Grades[I]
```

4.3.3 Array elements

Most actions to be undertaken with arrays are expressed, naturally, as subscript operations:

```
second := Grades[1]   -- for a BYTE variable second
```

However where sections of arrays are involved it is more succinct to express the operations as acting upon slices or segments of the array rather than individual elements. Moreover, slice operations can be implemented more efficiently. For example rather than have:

```
SEQ I = 7 FOR 10
  A[I]:= B[I - 7]
```

A slice operation would be:

```
[A FROM 7 FOR 10]:= [B FROM 0 FOR 10]
```

Note, that the square brackets are necessary but that the bounds (7 and 16, and 0 and 9, in the above example) can be dynamic. However, the lower bound must be non-negative and the upper bound greater than zero.

Array slices are particularly important when a series of elements is to be communicated down a channel. Here again considerable efficiency improvements can be obtained, however the channel must be 'informed' that such block communication is taking place. This is achieved by defining protocols and is described in the next chapter.

A further method of accessing an array is to use a table. A table has the same number of components as the array (or slice) and is contained within square brackets, for example:

```
[8]INT A:
SEQ
  A := [ao,a1,a2,a3,a4,a5,a6,a7]
    -- where ai is an integer variable that has
    -- a value at this point in the program
  [b1,b2] := [A FROM 4 FOR 2]
    -- bi is an INT variable
```

One of the effects of this code will be to set b1 to a4 and b2 to a5.

It follows from the syntax that a constant array is just a special case of a table.

Occam array structures are designed for ease of programming and efficiency of implementation. Arrays can be accessed by subscripts in the usual way. However groups of elements can be manipulated within a single expression by the use of slices (also called segments) and tables. Moreover complete array assignments are possible between arrays of the same structure. All of these group assignments can take advantage of block memory transfer instructions of the transputer (and other microprocessors) and block communication down a link between transputers.

4.4 Type definition

Although type definitions are not presently supported in occam, they may be included in future versions of the language. As is customary in languages like Pascal, a type name is defined by:

```
definition = TYPE name IS type :
```

Although new user defined types are not allowed a type definition can be used as an abbreviation for primitive types, array types and record types. Examples of usage are:

```
TYPE SYS.INT IS INT16:
TYPE SYS.REAL IS REAL32:

TYPE Count IS [16]INT:

VAL INT N IS 10:
TYPE MATRIX IS [N][N]REAL64:

TYPE String IS [1024]BYTE:
TYPE Page IS [64]String:
TYPE Book IS [250]Page:
```

Type definitions are used in the same way as predefined types in the declaration of variables:

```
SYS.INT I,J,K:

Count Vec:

MATRIX Results, Parameters:

Book Programming.In.Occam:
```

4.5 Record and variant types

The designers of occam have considered introducing records and variant records into the language. To this end a number of syntactical forms have been experimented with. Although these types are not presently supported, they may also be included in future versions of the language. A possible syntax for records is given below.

Records are used to define structures, the components of which may be of different types. Although records are undoubtedly useful programming tools, the motivation for including them in occam is more to do with communicating groups of objects down channels (and links) rather than general computation. A record is declared by first defining its type using a RECORD definition. For example:

```
RECORD INT.AND.REAL IS (INT,REAL32):

RECORD Odd.Collection IS (INT,BOOL,BYTE,REAL64):
```

Records are, in general, distinguished from arrays by the use of round, rather than square, brackets.

```
record type = ({,type})
```

where {,type} means one or more types separated by commas. In the above examples INT.AND.REAL defines a record type with two components, one INT and one REAL32. The other type definition, Odd.Collection, has four components all of different types.

Variables of these record types can be defined and used in assignments:

```
RECORD INT.AND.REAL IS (INT,REAL32):
INT.AND.REAL IR1,IR2:
INT I:
REAL32 R:
SEQ
  IR1 := (1,0.0)
  IR2 := IR1
  (I,R) := IR2
```

The constructs within brackets are record elements; (1,0.0) is a constant record, whereas (I,R) contains two variables (of appropriate type). The effect of executing this code is to set I to 1 and R to 0.0.

In occam there is no means of addressing a single component of a record in isolation from the whole structure. Therefore to add, say, one to the INT field of the above record (IR1) requires the record to be split up into its constituent parts and then reassembled after the field update:

```
INT I:
REAL32 R:
SEQ
  (I,R) := IR1
  I := I + 1
  IR1 := (I,R)
```

Although Pascal and Ada programmers will be used to updating individual components of records the lack of this provision in occam simplifies the implementation of records without removing any functionality from the language.

Further examples of record types are given below:

```
RECORD Three.INTs IS (INT,INT,INT):
RECORD Three.REALs IS (REAL32,REAL32,REAL32):

RECORD Threes IS (Three.INTs,Three.REALs):
  -- this record is composed of two records types

VAL INT Number.of.Names IS 64:
TYPE String IS [8]BYTE:
RECORD NAME IS (INT,String,String):
TYPE LIST IS [Number.of.Names]NAME:
```

With this last structure (which is an array of records) a new NAME (with index, say, 42) could be added to the array alist (of type LIST) as follows:

```
LIST alist:
NAME aname:
SEQ
  ...
  aname := (42,"    ALAN","    BURNS")
  alist[42] := aname
```

CHAPTER 5

Channel Protocols

A major criticism of earlier versions of occam (see Appendix E) was that data communication between processes could only take place a single object at a time. If ten integers had to be passed down a channel then ten distinct rendezvous were needed. This inevitably led to inefficiencies. It was also at variance with the transputer's capabilities (see Chapters 7 and 8), which could cope with block transfer down an inter-transputer link. Block transfer between processes on the same processor is, by comparison with link communication, straightforward. The current version of occam does allow groups of objects to be transferred during a single rendezvous. Moreover the primitive data types now supported in occam vary in length. It is therefore necessary to check the size of single objects during communication. Finally, type checking requirements force a channel to be 'aware' of the type of the input expression and output variable.

If groups of objects are to be transferred together then it is necessary for a program to be unambiguous in its use of channels. For example if ten BYTES are to be written to a channel, by some process, then exactly ten BYTES must be read. If less were read then there would, inevitably, be a run-time error. Communication down transputer links would be particularly difficult to arrange if both communicating partners did not know the size of the data being transferred.

To avoid run-time errors and inefficiencies it is necessary to build into the language features that will allow the compiler to check for erroneous programs. Apart from the simplest use of channels it is not possible for a compiler to check all block transfers and guarantee correct usage. Instead, occam has now added protocols to the definition of channels.

```
channel type = CHAN OF Protocol
```

Both input and output operations must be compatible with the defined protocol. If either is not then the compiler will reject the program or, in complex situations where the protocol is non-trivial, a well defined run-time error is specified with the usual effect of a process (or processes) being made equivalent to STOP.

A protocol is a statement about the type of the object using the channel. In the last chapter it was noted that occam supports primitive types and structured types. Protocols themselves can take one of three forms

```
definition =  PROTOCOL name IS simple protocol:
            | PROTOCOL name IS sequential protocol:
            | PROTOCOL name
                CASE
                  {tagged protocol}:
```

Each of the three forms will be considered in turn.

5.1   Simple protocols

A simple protocol is used to pass a single object (a primitive or structured type) down a channel. Its definition however also incorporates the transfer of a variable length array.

```
simple protocol =   type
                  | type::[]type

input = channel ? input item

input item =   variable
             | variable :: variable

output = channel ! output item

output item =   expression
              | expression :: expression
```

A simple protocol need not be explicitly defined; it can be used directly in the definition of the channel.

5.1.1   Primitive types

A primitive protocol is merely a simple scalar type, for example the familiar integer channel that has been used often in this book:

```
CHAN OF INT C1:
```

The input operation

```
C1 ? I
```

is compatible with the protocol provided I is of type INT. Similarly the output process:

```
C1 ! X
```

is compatible with the protocol as long as the expression X is of type INT.

Primitive protocols of this form can be defined for BOOL, BYTE and all the real types.

5.1.2   Array types

In the above example C1 is defined to pass simple integer values, one at a time. If, however, the programmer wishes to communicate a group of integers down a channel then it is more appropriate to define the channel to have either an array or a record protocol (or a sequential protocol – see next section). For example suppose that two processes always communicate five INT values (constructed as either a five element array or five distinct variables) with a primitive protocol this would involve five distinct rendezvous:

```
-- Example 1 using an array
CHAN OF INT C1:
PAR
  [5]INT OUT:
  SEQ
    -- generate OUT
    SEQ I = 0 FOR 5
      C1 ! OUT[I]
  [5]INT IN:
  SEQ
    SEQ J = 0 FOR 5
      C1 ? IN[J]
    -- use IN

-- Example 2 using 5 INT variables
CHAN OF INT C1:
PAR
  INT OUT1,OUT2,OUT3,OUT4,OUT5:
  SEQ
    -- generate OUT1 ... OUT5
    SEQ
      C1 ! OUT1
      C1 ! OUT2
      C1 ! OUT3
      C1 ! OUT4
      C1 ! OUT5
  INT IN1,IN2,IN3,IN4,IN5:
  SEQ
    SEQ
```

```
      C1 ? IN1
      C1 ? IN2
      C1 ? IN3
      C1 ? IN4
      C1 ? IN5
    -- use IN1 ... IN5
```

Considerable improvements in both readability and implementational efficiency can be obtained if instead of a simple primitive protocol a structured one is used:

```
CHAN OF [5]INT C5:
```

The two examples given above then reduce to:

```
  -- Example 1 using an array and an array protocol
  CHAN OF [5]INT C5:
  PAR
    [5]INT OUT:
    SEQ
      -- generate OUT
      C5 ! OUT
    [5]INT IN:
    SEQ
      C5 ? IN
      -- use IN

  -- Example 2 using 5 INT variables and an array protocol
  CHAN OF [5]INT C5:
  PAR
    INT OUT1,OUT2,OUT3,OUT4,OUT5:
    SEQ
      -- generate OUT1 ... OUT5
      C5 ! [OUT1,OUT2,OUT3,OUT4,OUT5]
    INT IN1,IN2,IN3,IN4,IN5:
    SEQ
      C5 ? [IN1,IN2,IN3,IN4,IN5]
      -- use IN1 ... IN5
```

In both of these examples the objects being input and output are compatible with the protocol definition because they form a five element INT array – either explicitly using an actual array or implicitly using a table.

Clearly arrays and tables can be mixed and array slices (as long as the size of the slice is correct) can be used. For example the following are all compatible with the protocol definition of the channel C5:

```
C5 ! [OUT1,OUT2,OUT3,OUT4,OUT5]
and
C5 ? IN
```

```
C5 ! [4,8,16,32,64]
and
C5 ? IN

C5 ! OUT
and
C5 ? [BIG.IN FROM 5 FOR 5]
```

where BIG.IN is an INT array of at least 10 elements

In all of the above examples the arrays being communicated have only had a small number of elements. Where large groups of objects need to be exchanged between processes (which may be executing on different processors) significant increases in speed (on the transputer at least) are observed if the exchange is expressed as a single communication using an appropriate protocol. For instance the following program outline involves the passing of over one million REAL64 values:

```
VAL INT N IS 1024:
CHAN OF [N][N]REAL64 Exchange:
PAR
  SEQ
    ...
    Exchange ? A
    ...
  SEQ
    ...
    Exchange ! B
    ...
```

where A and B are of type [N][N]REAL64.

5.1.3 Variable length arrays

In all the above examples a complete array was transferred down the channel. This is, in general, not always required; often only a proportion of the array need be communicated. The second form for a sequential protocol caters for this requirement:

```
simple protocol = type::[]type

input item = variable :: variable

output item = expression :: expression
```

For example the following defines a channel, VLA, that will pass up to 256 elements of a REAL32 array:

```
CHAN OF BYTE::[]REAL32 VLA:
```

A communication down VLA involves first sending a value (of type BYTE) to indicate the number of REAL32 values that will follow. The definition of the protocol therefore has to involve two types; the type of the count value – typically BYTE or INT – and the type of the array elements. Usage of VLA is straightforward; for example the following passes the first 17 elements of the array A to elements 20–36 in array B:

```
VLA ! 17::[A FROM 0 FOR 17]

VLA ? bt::[B FROM 20 FOR bt]
```

bt is of type BYTE and gets the value 17 after the rendezvous; A and B are appropriately sized REAL32 arrays.

5.1.4   Record types

The definition of a channel protocol can incorporate any valid occam type definition; it follows therefore that records, if provided, can also be communicated as a single entity. This is useful when the group of objects that should logically be transmitted together are of different type. As with array protocols a channel defined to have a record protocol can be used to transmit actual records or record elements:

```
RECORD INT.AND.REAL IS (INT,REAL32):
CHAN OF INT.AND.REAL Transmit:
PAR
  INT.AND.REAL IR1:
  INT I:
  REAL32 R:
  SEQ
    Transmit ? IR1
    ...
    Transmit ? (I,R)
    ...
  INT.AND.REAL IR2:
  SEQ
    ...
    Transmit ! (42,45.6)
    ...
    Transmit ! IR2
```

In this example a simple record type is defined (it contains only two components), a channel is declared to have this record type as its protocol and it is then used for two communications. With the first communication two literals are output in the second process and read into a variable IR1 (of type INT.AND.REAL) in the first process. This is followed by the values contained in IR2 being passed to the the variables I and R.

More complex record types are communicated in the same way as the above simple cases. Consider a record that contains a square matrix, its determinant, its inverse and two labels, one a string and the other an integer:

```
VAL INT N IS 24:
VAL INT String.Max IS 16:
TYPE MATRIX IS [N][N]REAL32:
TYPE String IS [String.Max]BYTE:
RECORD Matrix.Construct IS
   (INT,String,MATRIX,REAL32,MATRIX):
```

A channel for communicating these structures is defined and used as follows:

```
CHAN OF Matrix.Construct A.Channel:
PAR
  Matrix.Construct MC1:
  SEQ
    ...
    A.Channel ? MC1
    ...

  Matrix.Construct MC2:
  SEQ
    ...
    A.Channel ! MC2
    ...
```

As any input operation is allowed in a guard for an ALT process it follows that the input of a structures type would also be allowed:

```
VAL INT M IS 42:   -- some appropriate value
[M]CHAN OF Matrix.Construct A.Set:
PAR
  [M]Matrix.Construct MC:
  SEQ
    ...
    ALT I = 0 FOR M
      A.Set[I] ? MC[I]
        -- action
    ...
  ...
```

5.2   Sequential protocols

Arrays and records can be used to communicate groups of objects down channels as a single logical transaction. A sequential protocol allows such groups to be communicated without the use of structured types. Rather than have a simple protocol, of a structured type, a sequential protocol gives the types of each object being transferred:

```
sequential protocol = {; simple protocol}

input = channel ? {; input item}

output = channel ! {; output item}
```

An output

```
C ! X1 ; X2 ; X3 ; ... ; Xn
```

is compatible with the protocol

```
P1 ; P2 ; P3 ; ... ; Pn
```

provided that X_j is compatible with P_j. Similarly the input

```
C ? Y1 ; Y2 ; Y3 ; ... ; Yn
```

is compatible with the protocol provided Y_j is compatible with P_j.

A sequential protocol has to be defined before it is used in the declaration of a channel. To illustrate the use of this kind of protocol consider the transfer of five integers down channel ch:

```
PROTOCOL fiveint IS INT;INT;INT;INT;INT:
CHAN OF fiveint ch:
PAR

    ch ! out1;out2;out3;out4;out5
        -- all INT

    ch ? in1;in2;in3;in4;in5
        -- all INT
```

Similarly to send two objects of different type would involve:

```
PROTOCOL int.real IS INT;REAL32:
CHAN OF int.real ch:
PAR
```

```
ch ! outint ; outreal

ch ? inint ; inreal
```

5.3   Variant protocols

With all the above protocols the type of the object (or sequence of objects) is fixed by the definition of the channel. This is, in general, too rigid. Two processes may wish to pass data of various types and in no particular order. Consider two processes that exchange INT and REAL32 values; with a fixed protocol it would be necessary to define and use two channels;

```
CHAN OF INT C1:
CHAN OF REAL32 C2:
PAR
  SEQ
    -- first process; includes processes such as
    C1 ! I  -- integer
    C2 ! R  -- real
  SEQ
    -- second process, includes processes such as
    C1 ? J  -- integer
    C2 ? X  -- real
```

This 'solution' is clearly expensive in terms of channel definitions and could lead to deadlock problems or at least programs that are difficult to read and analyse. Occam removes the need to have a collection of channels between processes by providing variant protocols. A single channel can thus be used for all communication between two processes.

```
definition = PROTOCOL name
                CASE
                  {tagged protocol}
              :
tagged protocol =  tag
                 | tag ; protocol
tag = name
```

To output a variant type is straightforward. The channel is defined to have the correct variant protocol and the tag is used to indicate which variant is being output on each occasion the channel is used:

```
output = channel ! tag {; output item}
```

In the following example the channel C.all is used to communicate an integer or a REAL32 value:

```
PROTOCOL INT.OR.REAL
   CASE
      Fixed ; INT
      Float ; REAL32
   :
CHAN OF INT.OR.REAL C.all:
PAR
   SEQ
      -- first process, including processes such as
      C.all ! Fixed ; I  -- integer
      C.all ! Float ; R  -- real
```

Input of a value from a channel defined to have a variant protocol is more complicated. The reading process does not know the type of the object being transmitted, it must therefore have a collection of possible read actions; one for each tag field. This need is expressed in the syntax as an input selection or CASE structure:

```
case input = channel ? CASE
                {variant}

variant = tagged list
             process
           | specification:
             variant

tagged list = tag {; input item}

process = case input

alternative = case input
```

Note that the CASE structure not only provides a selector for each tag field but allows an arbitrary process to be executed after the variant type has been read. This enables algorithms that require different processing to be undertaken, depending on the type on the object being read, to be easily expressed. However, if the associated process would be SKIP and there is only one tagged list a shorthand form for the input is allowed:

```
input = channel ? CASE tagged list
```

The INT or REAL32 program can now be completed. In the code that is given below the reading process sets a Boolean flag (It.Was.An.Integer) to 'remember' which type of object was read.

```
PROTOCOL INT.OR.REAL
   CASE
      Fixed ; INT
      Float ; REAL32
```

```
    :
CHAN OF INT.OR.REAL C.all:
PAR
  SEQ
    -- first process, including processes such as
    C.all ! Fixed ; I  -- integer
    C.all ! Float ; R  -- real
  SEQ
    -- second process, including a process such as
    C.all ? CASE
      Fixed ; J
        It.Was.An.Integer := TRUE
      Float ; X
        It.Was.An.Integer := FALSE
```

An execution of the CASE input would either read an INT value into J (and set It.Was.An.Integer to TRUE) or a REAL32 value into X (and thereby set It.Was.An.Integer to FALSE). Exactly one of these actions will take place before the CASE input process terminates.

The input selection should have a tag value for each of the variants defined in the type. If having read a variant object there is no component with the same identifying tag then the selection behaves like STOP.

Clearly more complicated variant types are possible and will be communicated in the same manner.

Earlier in this chapter a simple protocol was used to pass a variable length array down a channel. If the lengths of the arrays being passed are restricted to a few possibilities then it may be more efficient to use a variant protocol:

```
PROTOCOL Variable.Array
  CASE
    short; [16]REAL32
    medium; [64]REAL32
    long; [2056]REAL32
  :
```

Consider, for illustration, a process that normalizes an object of type Variable.Array. By normalize we mean divide each element by the sum of all the elements. The process obtains the arrays down channel To.Normalize and passes the normalized form on to channel Has.Normalized. To update the data a long array hold is used; however, the type model requires arrays of correct size to be used when inputting the smaller variants. These temporary arrays are called hold1 and hold2.

```
[16]REAL32 hold1:    -- temporary array for short
[64]REAL32 hold2:    -- temporary array for medium
[2056]REAL32 hold:   -- array for data
INT size:
```

```
REAL32 sum:
WHILE TRUE
  SEQ
    sum:= 0.0
    To.Normalize ? CASE
      short; hold1
        SEQ
          size := 16
          [hold FROM 0 FOR size] := hold1
      medium; hold2
        SEQ
          size := 64
          [hold FROM 0 FOR size] := hold2
      long; hold
        size := 2056
    SEQ I = 0 FOR size
      sum := sum + hold[I]
    SEQ I = 0 FOR size
      hold[I] := hold[I]/sum
    IF
      size = 16
        SEQ
          hold1 := [hold FROM 0 FOR size]
          Has.Normalized ! short; hold1
      size = 64
        SEQ
          hold2 := [hold FROM 0 FOR size]
          Has.Normalized ! medium; hold2
      size = 2056
        Has.Normalized ! long; hold
```

Note that the tag field is a name not a data value, it is therefore not possible to assign a variable to the appropriate tag field and use it in the output to channel Has.Normalized. This is an unfortunate restriction and will at times lead to verbose code.

The last portion of the above code would have been more correctly expressed as a CASE structure. However to remove possible confusion between the CASE input and the CASE structure an IF was used. The code should have been expressed as follows:

```
CASE size
  16
    SEQ
      hold1 := [hold FROM 0 FOR size]
      Has.Normalized ! short; hold1
  64
    SEQ
      hold2 := [hold FROM 0 FOR size]
```

```
        Has.Normalized ! medium; hold2
   2056
        Has.Normalized ! long; hold
```

The final topic to consider with variant protocols is their use in an ALT process. The semantics required are straightforward; the input from a variant record should be allowed to form one, or more, of the alternatives in an ALT:

```
alternative = case input
```

For example, in the program just given, it would be possible to extend the capabilities of the normalizing process so that it not only read the variant type but could deal with, say, a fixed sized object coming down channel To.Also.Normalize:

```
[16]REAL32 hold1:   -- temporary array for short
[64]REAL32 hold2:   -- temporary array for medium
[128]REAL32 hold3:  -- new temporary array
[2056]REAL32 hold:  -- array for data
INT size:
REAL32 sum:
WHILE TRUE
  SEQ
    sum:= 0.0
    ALT
      To.Also.Normalize ? hold3
        SEQ
          size := 128
          [hold FROM 0 FOR size] := hold3
      To.Normalize ? CASE
        short; hold1
          SEQ
            size := 16
            [hold FROM 0 FOR size] := hold1
        medium; hold2
          SEQ
            size := 64
            [hold FROM 0 FOR size] := hold2
        long; hold
          size := 2056
    -- etc
```

5.3.1 CHAN OF ANY

If a channel is defined to have a protocol of ANY then all possible uses of the channel are compatible with its definition. In other words the compiler does not check on the channel's use and run-time errors will occur if the channel is misused. The occam programmer is not recommended to use this feature; however for obscure historical reasons the channel that is mapped to the screen must be defined to have this protocol:

```
CHAN OF ANY screen:
PLACE screen AT 1:
```

5.4   Language alternatives

Channel protocols, although necessary, are perhaps the least satisfactory feature of occam. They seem verbose and complicated to understand and use. Their complexity is due in part to the lack of appropriate data types; which results, for example, in variant objects being communicated even though variant records (or the equivalent) are not supported in the language.

The examples given earlier in this chapter make it clear that sequential protocols are not necessary if records (variables and elements) are provided. Sequential protocols are only needed because the record type may not be supported in all implementations of occam 2. If a future version of the language has a more complete set of data types, including records and variant records, then the protocol model would become much simpler. Indeed in this circumstance all channels would be declared to be of a single type and the protocol concept (in terms of being visible in the language syntax) could be removed.

CHAPTER 6

Abbreviations, Procedures and Functions

The only form of modularity supported in occam is the procedure; represented by the reserved word PROC. PROCs can be defined at any place where a variable declaration is allowed. A PROC may therefore be defined within a PROC, although recursive (and mutual recursive) declarations are not legal. PROCs are re-entrant in the sense that more than one process can call them concurrently as long as there are no 'global variables' manipulated within the PROC. Functions are also available in occam but they are constructed in such a way that they cannot give rise to side-effects.

Occam procedures and functions can, of course, have parameters; the rules regarding parameter association are however expressed in terms of abbreviations, which will therefore be considered first in this chapter.

6.1 Abbreviations

Occam is a block structured language; where a block is defined as:

```
block = specification
          scope

scope = process

specification =   declaration
              |  abbreviation
              |  definition
```

Declarations were considered in Chapter 4; definitions are described in the following sections.

Abbreviations allow a variable to be associated with the name or value of another variable (or expression). The abbreviation

```
INT i IS X:
```

means that i is a local name for X; it is a reference to X, therefore within the scope (of this abbreviation) a change to the value of i will also cause X to change; i is defined to be of type INT, thus X must also be INT. A formal way of expressing this abbreviation is

```
S n IS e = P(e)
  P(n)
```

where S is a type specifier and P is a process. P(e) is a process that depends on (uses) e; P(n) is the same process but depending on n; e.g.

```
INT new IS old:   =  SEQ
SEQ                  in ? old
  in ? new           out ! old
  out ! new
```

where in and out are INT channels

The abbreviation is invalid if n is used in P(n) after any action that changes e. However if P(n) contains no reference to e then the abbreviation is always valid as long as it is type compatible.

An example of the use of this abbreviation would be in the manipulation of an array element. The following code

```
[M][N]REAL32 MATRIX:
SEQ I = 0 FOR M
  SEQ J = 0 FOR N
    SEQ
      ch1 ? MATRIX[I][J]
      MATRIX[I][J] := MATRIX[I][J] * (MATRIX[I][J] + 42.0)
      ch2 ! MATRIX[I][J]
```

can be expressed (equivalently) as

```
[M][N]REAL32 MATRIX:
SEQ I = 0 FOR M
  SEQ J = 0 FOR N
    REAL32 EL IS MATRIX[I][J]:
    SEQ
      ch1 ? EL
      EL := EL * (EL + 42.0)
      ch2 ! EL
```

However, the following is invalid because of the rule specified earlier:

```
[M][N]REAL32 MATRIX:
SEQ I = 0 FOR M
  SEQ J = 0 FOR N
```

```
REAL32 EL IS MATRIX[I][J]:
SEQ
  ch1 ? EL
  MATRIX[I][J] := EL * (EL + 42.0)
      -- This an error - MATRIX[I][J]
      -- is being used after the abbreviation
  ch2 ! EL
```

Note that in this example if the type specifier has not been given:

```
EL IS MATRIX[I][J]:
```

then EL is automatically allocated the same type as MATRIX[I][J]. It is acceptable notation for:

```
S n IS e
```

to be written as:

```
n IS e
```

although the extra security provided by the compiler check that e is of type S has been lost.

The above discussion assumes that e, the element in the abbreviation, is a single variable. It is however possible for it to be an array:

```
[10]INT Mat IS VEC:
```

where VEC is of type [10]INT, or

```
[]INT Mat IS VEC:
```

In this case VEC can be any one dimensional array of INT.

Abbreviations can also be used with channels. In Section 3.5.2 a ten element buffer was given:

```
VAL INT N IS 10:
[N + 1]CHAN OF INT C:
PAR
  PAR P = 0 FOR N
    INT BufferElement:
    WHILE TRUE
      SEQ
        C[P] ? BufferElement
        C[P + 1] ! BufferElement
```

More efficient code can be generated if each array index is calculated only once rather than every time the channel is used:

```
VAL INT N IS 10:
[N + 1]CHAN OF INT C:
PAR
  PAR P = 0 FOR N
    INT BufferElement:
    in IS C[P]:
    out IS C[P + 1]:
    WHILE TRUE
      SEQ
        in ? BufferElement
        out ! BufferElement
```

The other form for an abbreviation (which was illustrated earlier) is to define a constant:

```
VAL S name IS expression:
```

where S is again a type specifier. For example:

```
VAL INT Max IS 1024:
VAL BOOL Go IS TRUE:
VAL REAL32 pi IS 3.14159267:
```

The expression can involve variables:

```
VAL INT Start IS First.Value + 1:
VAL INT Upper.Limit IS Max − 1:
```

As with the earlier form of abbreviation, the type specifier can be omitted if the type of the expression is unambiguous:

```
VAL Go IS TRUE:
VAL Start IS First.Value + 1:
```

Again the meaning of the VAL abbreviation can be expressed by the relationship:

```
VAL S name IS exp = P(exp)
  P(name)
```

A constant array is obtained by:

```
VAL [4]INT Exp IS [1,2,4,8]:
```

The abbreviation structures within occam can be described by the following relationship (see Appendix B for a complete description of the syntax):

```
abbreviation  =  specifier name IS element:
              |  VAL specifier name IS expression:

specifier  =  primitive type
           |  [expression]specifier
           |  []specifier
```

In addition it was noted in Chapter 4 that an abbreviation for a type can be given in a type definition:

```
TYPE Standard.INT IS INT32:
```

6.2   Definitions

An implementation will normally represent variables using a fixed number of bytes or words of computer memory. The type model of occam will ensure that variables are only used in a manner consistent with their type. There are however situations where it is desirable to interpret a representation as a variable or value of a different type. This is accomplished by the use of a definition:

```
definition  =  specifier name RETYPES element:
            |  VAL specifier name RETYPES expression:
```

This definition is therefore similar to an abbreviation except that there is a type change. In particular a definition is invalid if it is used after an update to the value of the element.

To illustrate the use of retyping consider an input process that reads an INT down a channel and then wishes to access the variable as if it were an array of BYTES.

```
INT I:   -- 32 bit representation
[4]BYTE B:
SEQ
  in ? I
  [4]BYTE B RETYPES I:
  SEQ
    -- the array B can now be
    -- accessed as long as I is
    -- not used
```

Care must be taken when using retyping conversions as they will invariably lead to implementation dependent processes.

6.3   Occam procedures

Procedures in occam are named processes with parameters:

```
definition = PROC name ({,formal})
                  body
               :


formal =   specifier name
         | VAL specifier name


body = process
```

where {,formal} means any number of formal parameters (including none) separated by commas. The definition of a PROC, as it is a specification, is completed by a colon (:) as the only character on a line; the colon must be under the P in PROC.

An instance of that PROC entails naming it and presenting an equal number of appropriate actual parameters:

```
instance = name ({,actual})
actual =   element
         | expression
```

For example,

```
PROC ARRANGE (INT High,Low)
  -- rearrange parameters so that the first
  -- has the largest value
  INT Temp:
  IF
    High < Low
      SEQ
        Temp := High
        High := Low
        Low := Temp
    TRUE
      SKIP
:
INT Number1, Number2:
SEQ
  keyboard ? Number1
  keyboard ? Number2
  ARRANGE (Number1,Number2)
  screen ! Number1
  screen ! Number2
```

Any identifier which is neither a locally defined one (such as Temp above) or a formal parameter is said to be a 'free identifier'. A free identifier must be in scope at the place of the PROC declaration (this is analogous to global variables in other languages).

With a program that is canonical (i.e. no identifier is used more than once), the parameter association can be expressed formally using abbreviations. Let a PROC declaration have the following form:

```
PROC P(F0, F1, F2, ..., Fn)
  B
:
```

where B is the occam process representing the body of the procedure. Then an instance of the PROC:

```
P(A0, A1, A2, ..., An)
```

can be replaced by:

```
F0 IS A0:
F1 IS A1:
F2 IS A2:
Fn IS An:
B
```

The 'call' of the procedure is therefore replaced by the body of the procedure, preceded by a series of abbreviations. This formal view has the semantics of inline expansion. An implementation may, however, compile the procedure as a substitution, as above, or as a closed subroutine in the usual way.

6.3.1 PROC parameters

All formal parameters in a PROC must have their types specified, they are passed (as the discussion above showed) by reference. Pass by value can be forced by including the term VAL in the parameter declaration:

```
PROC Maximum (VAL INT A, B, INT Max)
  IF
    A > B
      Max := A
    TRUE
      Max := B
:
```

Formally the parameter association, for a VAL parameter, is:

```
VAL Fi IS Ai:
```

With a VAL formal parameter the actual parameter may take the form of an expression; it acts as a constant within the procedure.

Arrays may be passed as parameters by including [] in the declaration of the formal parameter. The size of the array does not have to be given as any array (of the correct type and dimension) can be matched. This feature, combined with the use of the SIZE operator, allows general purpose procedures to be written. The following PROC can be used to find the average of any one dimensional real array:

```
PROC Average ([]REAL32 Data, REAL32 Res)
  SEQ
    Res := 0.0;
    SEQ i = 0 FOR SIZE Data
      Res := Res + Data[i]
    Res := Res/(REAL32 ROUND (SIZE Data))
  :
```

The expression Res/(REAL32 ROUND (SIZE Data)) means divide the real value Res by the length of the array Data, having first converted (by rounding) this length from INT to REAL32.

In all of the above examples the PROC parameters have been variables or values. There is however another important 'type' of parameter, namely channels. A channel or array of channels can be passed to a procedure in the same way as other objects. Consider, as an example, a PROC that concentrates the input from an array of channels (passing BYTE values) into a single out channel:

```
PROC Concentrator ([]CHAN OF BYTE IN, CHAN OF BYTE OUT)
  BYTE Element:
  WHILE TRUE
    ALT I = 0 FOR SIZE IN
      IN[I] ? Element
        OUT ! Element
  :
```

Note, that the protocol of the channel parameters must be given.

6.4   Use of PROCs

Clearly procedures, in all languages, are an important form of modularity. This is particularly true in occam if the PROCs do not have free identifiers. The standard programming support tools that surround occam can be used to develop programs as hierarchies of PROCs and some implementations may allow PROCs to be kept in different files and separately compiled. Libraries of PROCs are therefore a possibility and would have obvious advantages.

As a programming facility the use of PROCs can be subdivided into two, largely distinct, categories. Firstly, in a sequence of statements an instance of a PROC can be used (as a procedure is used in Pascal or Ada) to encapsulate part of that sequence. In this situation the parameters are usually variables (and values); for example, the Average PROC defined above. The second category consists of the use of a PROC to represent a subprocess of a PAR. Here the parameters are normally channels (and values). An example of this usage is the Concentrator PROC given at the end of the previous section. Within a PAR, the concurrent processes communicate by channels; a powerful design method is to specify each of these processes as a named PROC and to give their interfaces (the channels) as CHAN parameters to these PROCs.

For illustration consider, in outline, a simple program that takes the form of three processes in a line (this is known as a pipeline of processes). The three processes are represented by PROCs: First, Second and Third. Into First is passed a series of INTs from the keyboard; between the processes BYTEs are communicated and from the third INTs again emerge and are passed onto the screen. At the top level this program can be written as follows:

```
PROC First(CHAN OF INT in, CHAN OF BYTE out)
PROC Second(CHAN OF BYTE in,out)
PROC Third(CHAN OF BYTE in, CHAN OF INT out)
CHAN OF INT keyboard:
PLACE keyboard AT 2:
CHAN OF ANY screen:
PLACE screen AT 1:
CHAN OF BYTE ch1,ch2:
PAR
   First(keyboard,ch1)
   Second(ch1,ch2)
   Third(ch2,screen)
```

Because the bodies of the PROCs have not been given, this will not compile. However, by including a null (i.e. SKIP) process within the bodies of these PROCs the program becomes correct (syntactically) and the compiler can be used to check the logical consistency of the top level description of the program.

```
PROC First(CHAN OF INT in, CHAN OF BYTE out)
   SKIP
:
PROC Second(CHAN OF BYTE in,out)
   SKIP
:
PROC Third(CHAN OF BYTE in, CHAN OF INT out)
   SKIP
```

```
  :
CHAN OF INT keyboard:
PLACE keyboard AT 2:
CHAN OF ANY screen:
PLACE screen AT 1:
CHAN OF BYTE ch1,ch2:
PAR
    First(keyboard,ch1)
    Second(ch1,ch2)
    Third(ch2,screen)
```

Errors such as an incompatible interface between two processes can soon be isolated and corrected using this approach.

Having got the top level description correct each PROC can be coded. If any of these is still complicated the programmer is advised to further decompose the program in to subPROCs.

6.4.1 Prime number generator example

To illustrate this use of PROCs a non-trivial example will be given. This example is found in a number of books on concurrent programming and involves generating a sequence of prime numbers by using a sieve. The structure of the algorithm is given by Figure 6.1.

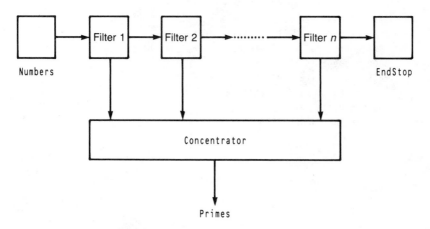

Figure 6.1 A prime number generator.

Each filter process obtains a prime number as the first integer it receives from its neighbour on the left. It is then passed a series of larger integers; if it can divide exactly any member of the series it discards it, otherwise it passes it on. In this way the first filter process will store the value 2, the second 3, the third 5 (4 being removed by the first filter), the fourth 7 etc.

To generate N prime numbers N filter processes are needed; having generated them the processes can be made to terminate by passing through zero.

At the top-most level the entire algorithm can be seen as a PROC to generate N primes (see Figure 6.2):

```
PROC Generate (CHAN OF INT Primes)
```

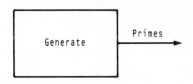

Figure 6.2 The generator process.

Within this PROC the structure represented by Figure 6.1 can be given in occam as:

```
VAL INT N IS 30:
PROC Generate ( CHAN OF INT Primes)
  VAL INT EndToken IS 0:
  PROC Filter (CHAN OF INT left, right, down)
  PROC Concentrator ([]CHAN OF INT in, CHAN OF INT out)
  PROC Numbers (CHAN OF INT in,out)
  PROC EndStop (CHAN OF INT in,out)
  [N + 1]CHAN OF INT InterFilter:
  [N]CHAN OF INT PC:
  CHAN OF INT OK.To.STOP:
  PAR
    Numbers (OK.To.STOP, InterFilter[0])
    PAR I = 0 FOR N
      Filter (InterFilter[I], InterFilter[I + 1], PC[I])
    EndStop (InterFilter[N],OK.To.STOP)
    Concentrator (PC, Primes)
  :
```

The above is not yet legal occam because the code for the bodies of the PROCs has not yet been given (although SKIPs could have been used to give a check). It illustrates, however, how the main PAR merely specifies a number of PROC instances to represent the necessary processes. The PROCs themselves have only channel parameters.

There remains the task of giving the code for each of the PROCs; first the simple PROC to generate the numbers:

```
PROC Numbers(CHAN OF INT in,out)
  INT i:
  SEQ
    i := 2
    WHILE i <> EndToken
      PRI ALT
        in ? i
          SKIP
        TRUE & SKIP
          SEQ
            out ! i
            i := i + 1
  :
```

Consider the development of this PROC; its main function is to generate an increasing series of integers, this could be done with an infinite loop:

```
INT i:
SEQ
  i := 2
  WHILE TRUE
    SEQ
      out ! i
      i := i + 1
```

To stop the sequence the value EndToken is passed down the channel in; therefore in each iteration a test must be made to see if there is a value waiting to be communicated down this channel:

```
INT i:
SEQ
  i := 2
  WHILE i <> EndToken
    SEQ
      out ! i
      i := i + 1
      ALT
        in ? i
          SKIP
        TRUE & SKIP
          SKIP
```

The ALT is needed so that the loop will continue if there is no value available on the input channel. However, as the guard TRUE & SKIP is always ready it could be chosen even when communication through in is possible. It follows that the ALT must be replaced by a PRI ALT that gives priority to the channel communication. A rearrangement of the code generates the PROC defined above.

Next, the code for the important Filter process is developed:

```
PROC Filter(CHAN OF INT left,right,down)
  INT p,q:
  SEQ
    left ? p
    q := 1    -- dummy value, not EndToken
    PAR
      down ! p
      WHILE q <> EndToken
        SEQ
          left ? q
          IF
            q = EndToken
              SKIP
            (q\p) <> 0
              right ! q
            TRUE
              SKIP
      right ! EndToken
  :
```

The concentrator takes values from the channel series and outputs them:

```
PROC Concentrator ([]CHAN OF INT in, CHAN OF INT out)
  INT p:
  SEQ i = 0 FOR N
    SEQ
      in[i] ? p
      out ! p
  :
```

Finally there is the procedure that gives the code for the process at the end of the filters:

```
PROC EndSTOP(CHAN OF INT in,out)
  INT temp:
  SEQ
    in ? temp
    PAR
      out ! EndToken
      WHILE temp <> EndToken
        in ? temp
  :
```

Once initiated this process becomes immediately suspended and remains in that state until some value appears down channel `in`. It then communicates `EndToken` down the `out` channel concurrent with reading more values from 'upstream'.

The complete program can thus be assembled and when executing it will generate the appropriate number of prime numbers before terminating.

As well as illustrating the use of `PROC`s to represent code that will be executed as a concurrent process, this example indicates the form a program must take if correct termination is to occur. Perhaps the greatest source of error in occam programs is the deadlock brought about by a faulty closing down sequence. In the above program only one process (`EndSTOP`) has responsibility for recognizing the condition appropriate for termination. It then communicates this to the head of all pipelines in the program (in this case there is only one; `Numbers`). The instruction to closedown is communicated, in the form of a token, down all pipes; with each process making sure it:

1. passes the token on, then

2. closes down, and

3. does not read upstream again after receiving the token.

The process that initiated the closedown then waits until the token (or tokens) it transmitted are returned, it can then terminate itself. Note that the sending out of the token and the continuous reading from upstream must be done in parallel. Otherwise a circular graph of dependencies may ensue which would itself lead to a deadlock.

If the above structure is used the graceful termination of all processes within a `PAR` will occur.

Finally this example shows the importance of using appropriate names for channel parameters. Compare the diagram for the `FILTER PROC` (Figure 6.3) and the specification of the `PROC` itself:

```
PROC FILTER(CHAN OF INT left,right,down)
```

The diagram has the important extra information that the direction of usage of the channels is indicated. The syntax of the `PROC` specification does not contain this information. If the `PROC` had been given as

```
PROC FILTER(CHAN OF INT one,two,three)
```

then any inconsistency in the top level description of the program would not be as easy to observe. It would only be later when the whole program was compiled together that the fault would be recognized. By using

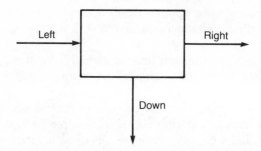

Figure 6.3 A filter process.

parameter names such as in and out informal information is being added to
the formal syntax.

6.5   Parallel searching

The following example illustrates the use of concurrency in the exploitation
of multiprocessor hardware. Sequential searching techniques abound,
with most being based on an initial sorting of the data. And yet for very
large data sets a significant reduction in search time can only be effectively
accommodated if the overall search is broken down into a collection of
smaller searches that can be undertaken simultaneously.

To achieve this, the processes are normally arranged as a tree, see
Figure 6.4.

As is usual with a 'computer' tree the leaves are at the bottom and the
branches are above them; the top-most branch is known as the 'root'. The
search routine therefore involves:

1. communicating a search key to root;
2. dispersing the key through the branches to all the leaves;
3. checking for the existence of the key in each leaf (in parallel);
4. gathering in the results from all the leaves, via the branches; and
5. communicating from root the result of the search.

To obtain an occam program for this search routine requires the development of two PROCs for the two process types – leaves and branches. In order
to simplify the code each leaf will be assumed to have only one data item
(Data) of type INT and the result passed up the tree will be a Boolean one,
merely indicating whether the key was found. The PROC for the branches is
as follows (six channel parameters are needed; two from the node above –

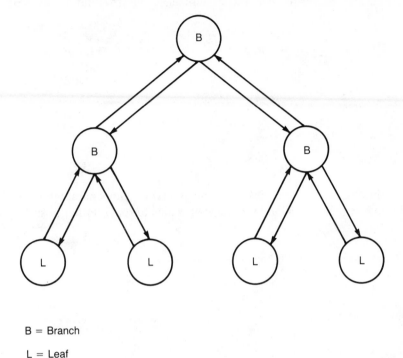

B = Branch

L = Leaf

Figure 6.4   A tree of processes.

req and ans, two to the node below left – Lreq and Lans, and two to the node below right – Rreq and Rans):

```
PROC branch(CHAN OF INT req,Lreq,Rreq, CHAN OF BOOL ans,Lans,Rans)
    WHILE TRUE
        INT key:
        BOOL al,ar:
        SEQ
            req ? key
            PAR
                Lreq ! key
                Rreq ! key
            PAR
                Lans ? al
                Rans ? ar
            ans ! al OR ar
    :
```

Interestingly, as the nature of the problem implies that a answer cannot be given before a request has been made, it is not necessary to force the key outputs and returns to be in a strict sequence. The SEQ could thus be written as:

```
SEQ
  req ? key
  PAR
    Lreq ! key
    Rreq ! key
    Lans ? al
    Rans ? ar
  ans ! al OR ar
:
```

The simpler PROC for leaf processes only has two channel parameters, one to obtain a request – req, and the other on which to reply (either positively or negatively):

```
PROC leaf(CHAN OF INT req, CHAN OF BOOL ans)
  INT Data,key:
  SEQ
    -- load data
    WHILE TRUE
      SEQ
        req ? key
        ans ! key = Data
:
```

To illustrate how a tree of processes can be set up consider a trivial example with four data items; i.e. four leaves and a tree with a depth of 3. To generate a tree of this depth requires 8 down and 8 up channels, see Figure 6.5.

The complete program is therefore:

```
[8]CHAN OF INT C:
[8]CHAN OF BOOL A:
PROC branch(CHAN OF INT req,Lreq,Rreq, CHAN OF BOOL ans,Lans,Rans)
  -- body of PROC
PROC leaf(CHAN OF INT req, CHAN OF BOOL ans)
  -- body of PROC
PROC User.Interface(CHAN OF INT out, CHAN OF BOOL in)
  -- body of some appropriate user interface process
PAR
  branch(C[1],C[2],C[3],A[1],A[2],A[3])
  branch(C[2],C[4],C[5],A[2],A[4],A[5])
  branch(C[3],C[6],C[7],A[3],A[6],A[7])
  PAR i = 4 FOR 4
    leaf(C[i],A[i])
  User.Interface(C[1],A[1])
```

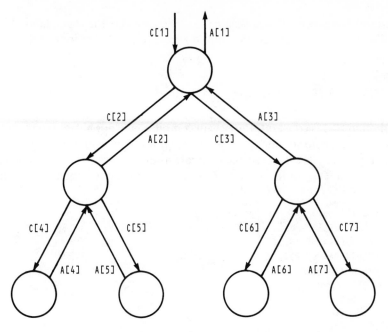

Figure 6.5   A tree of depth two.

The PAR replicator i = 4 FOR 4 sets up 4 processes; within each i has either the value 4, 5, 6 or 7.

The general solution for any depth of tree is given in the next program. If n is the depth of the tree then P[n] is the number of up and down channels needed and P[n - 1] is the number of leaf processes generated, where P[] is a constant vector of the form:

```
VAL [10]INT P IS [1,2,4,8,16,32,64,128,256,512]:
```

The general solution is therefore:

```
VAL INT n IS 8:   -- for example
VAL [10]INT P is [1,2,4,8,16,32,64,128,256,512]:
[P[n]]CHAN OF INT C:
[P[n]]CHAN OF BOOL A:
PAR
  PAR i = 0 FOR n - 1
    PAR j = 0 FOR P[i]
      branch(C[P[i]+ j ],C[P[i + 1]+(j * 2)],
             C[P[i + 1]+((j * 2) + 1)],
             A[P[i] + j],A[P[i + 1]+(j * 2)],
             A[P[i + 1] + ((j * 2) + 1)])
  PAR k = P[n - 1] FOR P[n - 1]
    leaf(C[k],A[k])
```

It was noted earlier that as occam is a static language the range field of a PAR replicator must be a constant. In the above program the inner PAR has the form:

```
PAR j = 0 FOR P[i]
```

Although P[i] is constant, the occam compiler may not be able to recognize this and will, consequently, reject the program. However as i clearly has an upper limit of n − 2 it is possible to create more processes than are necessary and allocate SKIP to the superfluous ones. The program thus becomes:

```
VAL INT n IS 8:    -- for example
VAL [10]INT P is [1,2,4,8,16,32,64,128,256,512]:
[P[n]]CHAN OF INT C:
[P[n]]CHAN OF BOOL A:
PAR
  PAR i = 0 FOR n − 1
    PAR j = 0 FOR P[n − 2]
      IF
        j <= P[i]
          branch(C[P[i] + j],C[P[i + 1] + (j * 2)],
                 C[P[i + 1] + ((j * 2) + 1)],
                 A[P[i] + j],A[P[i + 1] + (j * 2)],
                 A[P[i + 1] + ((j * 2) + 1)])
        TRUE
          SKIP
  PAR k = P[n − 1] FOR P[n − 1]
    leaf(C[k],A[k])
```

The advantage of using a tree structure of processes is that for each single increase in depth the number of leaf processes doubles. For example a tree of depth 8 has 128 leaves, whereas a depth of 16 generates over 32,000 leaves. Clearly the use of such high numbers of processors is beyond present capabilities. However, the potential for making use of parallel machines for searching through very large databases is significant.

6.6   Functions

One of the intended application areas for occam (and the transputer) is numerical analysis. Within this area the concurrency offered by occam coupled with the parallelism supplied by the transputer enables cost effective systems to be built whose performance is comparable with that of the powerful (and more expensive) supercomputers. One language feature that numerical analysts feel is necessary is the function. Some programmers in this domain would even argue that functions are a fundamental requirement if readable and expressive programs are to be written.

Unfortunately languages such as Pascal introduce the function in a way that undermines the semantics of other features of the language. The classic difficulty with functions is **side-effects**. This is where a function not only returns a result but changes the value of other variables that are in scope. Another hidden effect, that is possible in a concurrent programming language, is for a function to contain internal concurrency. The evaluation of a simple expression can, in these circumstances, lead to the creation and execution of processes with even the possibility of delay or deadlock occurring. It follows that the full meaning of any expression that contains a function call can only be inferred by examining the code for the function itself.

Occam introduces the function in a controlled way that prohibits side-effects but is sufficiently expressive to allow effective use. An example of a simple function is one that averages two REAL32 values:

```
REAL32 FUNCTION ave(VAL REAL32 A,B) IS (A + B) / FLOAT 2 :
```

The function is given a type and the structure after the IS is an expression of that type. Parameters must be VAL and the formal expression of parameter passing is the same as for PROCs. Again a function can be compiled to be a closed subroutine or a substitution of the expression.

Having defined the function it can be used in the usual way.

```
Z := ave(X,Y)
```

To calculate the average of three variables, given only this function would require a nested function call:

```
Z := ave(W, ave(X,Y))
```

As part of an expression the usual brackets must be used:

```
DIFF := X + (ave(X,Y)/Z)
```

This example represents the simplest form an occam function can take; the result is available immediately as a simple expression made up entirely of the parameters and a constant. In general a function may need to compute intermediate values before the final result can be obtained. These intermediate calculations, if necessary, are undertaken within the function's body which takes the form of a **valof**. A valof is an occam construct that defines a process whose behaviour is restricted to whatever actions are required before the value of an expression can be evaluated. The restrictions imposed on this process are such that side-effects cannot occur.

```
valof =    VALOF
              process
              RESULT expression list
         | specification
           valof
```

For example the simple average calculation could have been expressed as a series of intermediate stages:

```
Z := REAL32 Temp:
     VALOF
       SEQ
         Temp:= X
         Temp:= Temp + Y
         Temp:= Temp / FLOAT 2
       RESULT Temp
```

As part of a function the VALOF represents the body, or execution part:

```
REAL32 FUNCTION ave (VAL REAL32, A,B)
  REAL32 Temp:
  VALOF
    SEQ
      Temp:= A
      Temp:= Temp + B
      Temp:= Temp / FLOAT 2
    RESULT Temp
  :
```

Of course this code is extravagant and would actually be written as

```
REAL32 FUNCTION ave(VAL REAL32 A,B)
  VALOF
    SKIP
    RESULT (A + B) / FLOAT 2
  :
```

It is when the VALOF consists only of a SKIP process that the shortened version using the IS clause is permitted.

The VALOF is a construct in its own right but its use is primarily within the definition of a function. The restrictions on the process within a VALOF are critically important:

1. It must not contain a PAR construct.
2. It must not contain an ALT construct.
3. It must not contain channel input or output operations.

4. Any assignment must be to a variable defined within or just prior to the VALOF.

These restrictions remove the possibility of side-effects.

To give a more realistic example of a function (i.e. one that does not have a SKIP body) the following finds the statistical standard deviation of a series of observations. The observations are held as the first *N* values in an array called 'Observations'. Before giving this function however, two others that will be of use are defined:

```
REAL32 FUNCTION SQR(VAL REAL32 X) IS X * X:
-- gives the square of the parameter

REAL32 FUNCTION SQRT(VAL REAL32 X)
  REAL32 Sqroot:
  VALOF
    SEQ
      -- gives the square root of the parameter
      .
      .
      .
      RESULT Sqroot
  :
```

The standard deviation function can now be given as:

```
REAL32 FUNCTION Standard(VAL []REAL32 Obs, VAL INT N)
  REAL32 std:
  VALOF
    REAL32 Ave:
    SEQ
      Ave := 0.0
      std := 0.0
      SEQ i = 1 FOR N
        Ave := Ave + Obs[i]
      Ave := Ave / (REAL32 ROUND N)
      SEQ i = 1 FOR N
        std := std + SQR(Obs[i] — Ave)
      std:= SQRT(std)
      RESULT std
  :
```

6.6.1   Multi-value assignments and functions

Although the normal assignment has the form:

```
variable := expression
```

occam supports a multiple assignment operator that can be used in place of a sequence of individual assignments.

```
assignment = variable list := expression list
```

where *variable list* is a list of one or more variables separated by commas and *expression list* is an identical number of expressions. The variables (and hence the expressions) do not have to be of the same type. An example of the use of a multiple assignment is:

```
X,Y,Z := a,b,c
```

where a is an expression of the same type as X; similarly b and Y, and c and Z. This is equivalent to

```
SEQ
  X:= a
  Y:= b
  Z:= c
```

If the expression list contains some of the variables in the variable list then there could be confusion over the meaning of the multiple assignment. To ensure that the operator is unambiguous all the expressions are evaluated before any of the assignments are made. Hence the assignment:

```
X,Y,Z := X + 4, X + Z, X + Y
```

is equivalent to:

```
SEQ
  PAR
    t1:= X + 4
    t2:= X + Z
    t3:= X + Y
  X:= t1
  Y:= t2
  Z:= t3
```

(t1, t2 and t3 are local variables of the appropriate type).

One of the uses of the multiple assignment is that it enables the definitions of VALOF and functions to be generalized so that they also deal with expression lists rather than single values.

```
valof =   VALOF
            process
            RESULT expression list
```

```
|  specification
   valof

definition = {, type} FUNCTION name ({, format})
                   function body
             :
function body = valof
```

The function must have at least one type but it may have no formal (parameter) part. To illustrate the use of a multiple value function consider the standard deviation function given above. It can easily be changed to return both the standard deviation and average of the set of recorded observations.

```
REAL32, REAL32 FUNCTION Standard(VAL []REAL32 Obs, VAL INT N)
  REAL32 std, Ave:
  VALOF
   -- as before
  RESULT std, Ave
:
```

The use of this function must always take the form of a two-value assignment:

```
SD,A := Standard(Observations, N)
```

CHAPTER 7

The Transputer

As was indicated in Chapter 1 the development of the occam programming language has been undertaken alongside the design and construction of the transputer. In the next chapter the implementation of occam on the transputer is described. A short overview of the hardware is given in this chapter.

'Transputer' is a generic term describing a family of programmable VLSI devices including disk controllers, floating point processors, graphics processors, signal processing devices and 32-bit and 16-bit general purpose processors. A standard processor is illustrated in Figure 7.1; this transputer contains internal memory and four communication links for direct connection with other transputers. The address bus is, of course, joined to external memory and is implemented in such a way that there is a continuous address space including both internal and external memory. The first transputers were launched with 2 K bytes of on-chip memory; 4 K versions of the 32-bit transputer are also available and it is possible that 8 K devices will be produced.

The four links are connected to the main processor via four link interfaces. These interfaces can, independently, manage the communications of the link (including direct access to memory). As a result of this architecture a transputer can simultaneously communicate on all four links (in both directions) and execute an internal process. Much of the power of the transputer comes from this facility. Point-to-point communication, between processors, has the following advantages:

1. It does not require a fast communication bus.
2. Arbitrarily large systems can be constructed with all connections being local and short.
3. The communication medium does not saturate when extra processes are added.

4. Fault-tolerant systems can be constructed that do not depend on the reliability of the critically important bus.
5. Board layout is easier.

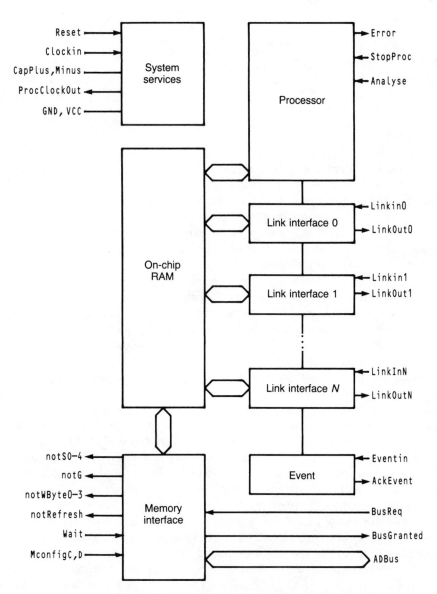

Figure 7.1   A schematic view of a transputer.

The main disadvantage with point-to-point communication is that messages being transferred between two processors may have to pass through a number of intermediary processors. Store and forward software can however be incorporated where necessary on each transputer:

```
SEQ
  MessageSource ? BufferA
  WHILE TRUE
    SEQ
      PAR
        MessageSource ? BufferB
        MessageSink ! BufferA
      PAR
        MessageSource ? BufferA
        MessageSink ! BufferB
```

In this code a message is first read into BufferA; after this, the process goes into an infinite loop where it executes a SEQ process. The first part of this SEQ involves writing out the value of BufferA concurrent with reading in a new value into BufferB. Once both of these actions have taken place the second part of the SEQ is executed. This reverses the actions (i.e. BufferB is output and BufferA is given a new value). If the two channels MessageSource and MessageSink are mapped onto links this process will pass on all the data it receives.

Each of the four links available on the standard transputers will implement two channels (in opposite directions). The link interfaces and the processor operate in parallel and each link interface can provide block transfer. A message consists of a sequence of bytes, and after each byte the sending transputer must wait for an acknowledgement. However, as the acknowledgement can be sent on receipt of the first bit an essentially continuous transmission can take place.

The other significant pins illustrated in Figure 7.1 are Error, Analyse, EventIn and ClockIn. A software error, such as numerical overflow causes the Error flag to be set; this could then be read by another transputer in the system. Recovery from the error condition can be achieved by use of Analysis which can be used to restart the processor, without affecting memory, using either an internally available or externally provided bootstrap program.

The EventIn pin (and the associated AckEvent) is a form of interrupt mechanism and can be mapped onto a channel within the executing occam program. The use of this pin is discussed further in Chapter 9.

ClockIn cycles at a standard 5 MHz; within the transputer this is stepped up to give a faster processing cycle and stepped down for use with TIMER channels (see next chapter).

7.1   The instruction set

The lowest level at which a transputer will normally be programmed is occam; the instruction set has therefore not been designed as a programming language but to enable simple and efficient compilation and execution. It consists of a relatively small number of instructions, all of which have the same basic format. The instruction set will be kept compatible over all transputer products.

Each instruction is only one byte long and contains a 4-bit value and a 4-bit function code; see Figure 7.2. This representation therefore allows for only 16 basic functions; thirteen of which are used to code the most important and frequently used functions of the computer. Such functions include: load constant, add constant, load local, store local, store non-local (non-local functions use the top of the evaluation stack as offset), jump, conditional jump, call, etc.

The three remaining codes are

```
operate
prefix
negative prefix
```

The function operate causes its data field (the operand) to be interpreted as an operation to be performed on the evaluation stack (the evaluation stack consists of three fast registers). As the operand field is only 4-bits wide this function, on its own, can distinguish between sixteen operations; again the most common arithmetic and comparison actions are encoded within this sixteen. To gain access to other operations this function must be preceded by a prefix, or negative prefix.

These last two functions allow the data field to be extended (indefinitely). With all the above instructions the first action taken, when that code is executed, is for the operand to be loaded into the least significant 4 bits of the operand register. The final action of all instructions (apart from prefix and negative prefix) is to clear this operand register ready for the next instruction. With the prefix function, however, the data field is shifted four places up the operand register and the register is not cleared. The

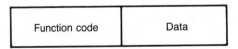

Figure 7.2   The transputer word.

effect of this is for the next instruction, after it has loaded its 4-bit operand, to be working on an 8-bit data value. Two preceding prefix instructions will yield a 12-bit data value; etc.

Negative prefix acts in the same way as prefix accept that the operand register is complemented before the data is shifted. These instructions enable operands with the range -256 to 255 to be constructed using only a single prefixing instruction.

Sections of occam programs that manipulate bytes, Boolean values and words can, as a result of the above structures, be translated into transputer instructions that are largely independent of word length.

Measurements and analysis have indicated that about 80% of code (generated from occam programs) can be executed without a prefix or negative prefix instruction. Moreover as the prefetch buffer can hold two words of memory (i.e. 8 instructions on the 32-bit transputer) it is rare for the processor to have to wait for an instruction fetch cycle before proceeding.

7.2   Physical properties

In order to give an impression of the transputer's performance the following statistics and characteristics may be useful:

- Each transputer is a single VLSI CMOS chip.
- On-chip memory is inherently fast static RAM.
- The 32-bit transputer gives access to 4 gigabytes of off-chip memory through a 32-bit wide multiplexed address/data bus.
- A transputer will function at a speed between 5 and 10 MIPS (Millions Instructions Per Second). Note, these are reduced instructions.
- The process cycle has a duration of 50 ns; a 25 ns cycle time is possible in the future.
- A link can transfer data at a rate of 10 or 20 megabits per second, again faster data transfer rates are possible.
- The design target for transmission failure on a link, due to a synchronization failure, is less than 0.1 FIT (less than one failure in ten thousand million device operating hours).
- Transputers with more that 4 links are now technically feasible.

Although a typical member of the transputer product family consists of a single chip containing processor, memory and communication links, the most powerful member of the family also contains an on-chip floating point unit (FPU). This 64-bit FPU operates concurrently with, but under the control of, the central processor. It is built upon a three deep floating point evaluation stack and forms a computing engine of considerable power; for example it is capable of sustaining well over one million floating point operations per second.

CHAPTER 8

Implementing Occam on the Transputer

In this chapter the mapping of occam programs on to the transputer is described. High performance is necessary if transputers are to be used in time-critical systems or if multi-transputer configurations are to challenge the speed of the supercomputers. Other concurrent programming languages have proved to be difficult to implement efficiently; in particular Ada (Burns, 1985) has serious difficulties here, requiring sophisticated compiler optimization techniques to obtain adequate performance. Occam has the advantage that an 'occam engine' is already available.

One element of this 'occam engine' is the provision of instructions that apply directly to the execution of occam programs. In the previous chapter the instruction set for the transputer was described; operations that support the process model include:

- start process,
- end process,
- input message,
- output message,
- delay process.

To execute the ALT process it is necessary to wait for one of a number of possible events. Instructions are available to accommodate this effectively. Other instructions support the reliable execution of sequential code, for example array bounds checking is always provided.

8.1 Support for sequential processes

The transputer processor has six registers available for use with a sequential process; see Figure 8.1. The registers A, B and C form the evaluation stack; the workspace register points to an area of store where local variables for the currently executing process are located; the next instruction register has the usual function and the operand register was described in the previous chapter. Expressions are evaluated on the stack; the designers of the transputer felt (after performing a statistical analysis) that a stack size of three provided the optimum balance between code compactness and implementation complexity. As occam is designed so that its compiler can recognize situations that would lead to stack overflow, no provisions are made on the transputer to deal with this overflow condition. This improves run-time efficiency.

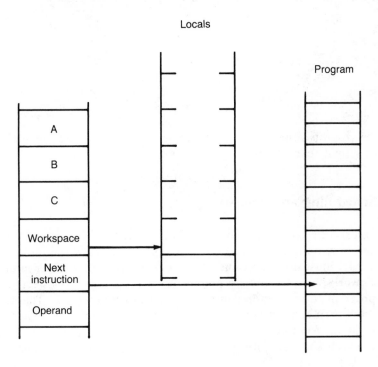

Figure 8.1   Support for sequential program structures.

The use of a workspace and next instruction register implies that there is no overhead in using a SEQ constructor. This is however not the case for PAR.

8.2   Support for concurrent processes

In Chapter 1 it was noted that a process can be in one of three states:

1. suspended,

2. executing, or

3. executable.

A process that is suspended is waiting for an input or output action to be completed on a channel (including delay on a TIMER). For each transputer in a system there will only be one executing process, all other processes that are able to execute must be kept on a dispatch queue. To this end two further registers are employed to implement concurrency. In Figure 8.2 this scheme is illustrated; the example shown is for the following PAR process:

```
PAR
  P
  Q
  R
  S
  T
```

where process T is suspended, R is executing and P, Q and S are executable (but not actually executing).

8.3   Scheduling and priority

When an executing process is no longer able to proceed (for example if it attempted to write to a channel on which a process was not waiting) then the scheduler must store the value of the 'next instruction' register in that process's workspace. The process pointed to, from the 'front' register, then has its program pointer restored into the next instruction register. This new process will then continue its execution (after the appropriate change to the value in the 'front' register has been made). When a suspended process becomes executable again it is placed on the back of the queue using the 'back' register.

The context switch involved in moving from running one process to executing another is very quick, due to three important factors:

1. The scheduler is a hardware facility.

2. When a process is suspended there are no values on the evaluation stack that need be stored (or restored when it is next executed).

3. The transputer has been designed to have a minimum number of shared registers; the on-chip RAM is effectively a collection of non-shared registers.

The second factor comes from the rule that a process cannot be suspended during the evaluation of an expression (which would use the stack). Even

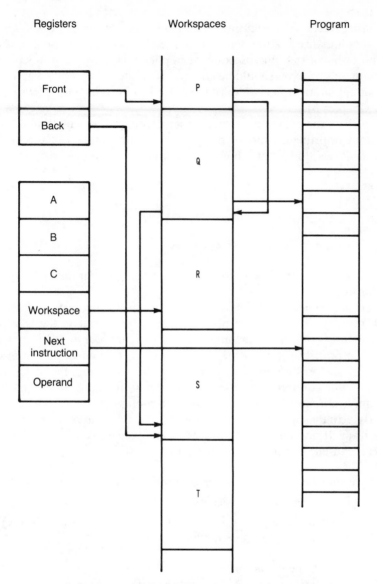

Registers   Workspaces   Program

Figure 8.2   Support for parallel program structures.

the appearance of an interrupt (EventIn) will not cause a process to be suspended whilst using the stack (see below). Together these factors provide the basis for an efficient occam-engine.

The workspace for the PAR process itself will keep a count of the number of non-terminated component subprocesses. As a process terminates it executes an 'end process' instruction that decrements this counter value.

It should be clear from the above description that the execution of a PAR process entails a run-time overhead. Queues must be set up and registers initialized. Although this overhead is not usually significant (it is of the order of one microsecond) it implies that a series of independent assignment processes should be coded as a SEQ not a PAR. Only where there is channel interaction should a PAR be used to introduce non-determinacy (see Chapter 3).

Earlier, the PRI PAR constructor was introduced as a method of giving different priorities to sets of processes. The transputer will support two priority levels; the PRI PAR should therefore only have two components:

```
PRI PAR
  PAR
    -- set of high priority processes
  PAR
    -- set of low priority processes
```

If there are more than two processes in a PRI PAR, all but the first is given a low priority.

To accommodate the priority levels there are two sets of front and back registers, one for each priority queue. Interestingly, the transputer implements two distinct scheduling algorithms for these two priority levels. If a high priority process is executable then it, of course, has preference over any low priority process. Moreover, once executing, the high priority process will continue to execute unless it terminates, stops, waits for communication, or delays. It cannot be pre-empted.

By comparison the low priority scheduler uses a round-robin algorithm. If no high priority processes are executable a low priority one will be chosen; it will then execute until:

- It terminates, stops, waits for communication, or delays.
- A high priority process becomes executable.
- It has been executing for between 1 and 2 timeslices (see below) and has reached the end of a control structure.

A timeslice will be of the order of 820 microseconds.

Each low priority process will therefore have a quantum of processing time before returning to the back of the executable queue. The scheduler is thus, in a broad sense, fair.

A low priority process can be pre-empted by a high priority one that was previously suspended but has become executable. This could occur if:

- It was delayed and the delay time has now expired.
- It was waiting to communicate with a low priority process that has now reached this point of communication.

- It was waiting to communicate with a process, running on a different transputer, that is now ready to communicate.

- It was waiting to synchronize with the channel mapped on to the EventIn pin (see previous chapter) and an interrupt has arrived.

In all these eventualities the currently executing low priority process will be suspended (at the next appropriate point) and the executable high priority process will be swapped in.

To enable real-time responsiveness to be checked the transputer gives an upper bound upon the time it takes for the low priority process to reach a point at which it can be suspended (without the need to save values on the evaluation stack). A typical maximum value here would be 40 processor cycles. In addition the time it takes to execute the context switch to the high priority process is calculable (typically 18 cycles if data and program are on on-chip memory). Together these figures give a measure of the maximum delay one might expect if servicing, say, an external interrupt. This, of course, pre-supposes that there is not a high priority process already executing!

By having the hardware directly implement a fixed scheduling scheme considerable improvements in speed of execution are obtainable. Against this one must balance the drawbacks of having a rigid system imposed upon the programmers, that they cannot change or even modify. One possible criticism of the model is that a high priority process, if it chooses to communicate with a low priority process, must wait until the round-robin scheme brings that process to the processor. Some programmers might prefer a model that would temporarily upgrade the low priority process to the higher level if such a communication is initiated (this would however be inefficient to implement). Other programmers may indeed object to having only two priority levels.

These criticisms about the rigidity of the transputer scheduling scheme must, nevertheless, be set within the context of the implementation of other concurrent programming languages. Such languages (e.g. Ada) require a run-time support system, that is usually supplied by the compiler, to provide the environment for the execution of the concurrent processes. It is usual for these run-time support systems to be similarly rigid and for the programmer again to have little control over the manner in which the program is actually executed. The transputer scheme is no more restrictive than those software systems; it is, however, considerably more effective.

8.3.1 TIMERs

It was described earlier how a value of a local real-time clock can be obtained within an occam program by defining a TIMER and reading from it. The transputer supports two timers, one for high priority processes and one for low priority processes. As the value of the local real-time clock is restricted to a fixed number of bits (the word length of the host processor) then there is a clear trade-off between the accuracy of the clock and the range of times supported.

For high priority processes the value of the clock increments every 5 cycles of the clock input. Typically this will mean that the timer has a resolution of one microsecond but will cycle round in just over 71 minutes on a 32-bit machine. It follows that the delay statement:

```
Time ? AFTER e
 -- where Time has been declared a TIMER
```

can accommodate a value of e of up to 35 minutes. The comparison between e and the local clock is performed using a modulo comparison to ensure a correct result.

To get an increased range, the resolution for low priority process is increased to 64 microseconds. The result is that a cycle of approximately 74 hours is available. A process can thus delay for up to 37 hours.

Processes that are delayed are placed on a single queue. The queue is ordered according to the time each process should become executable again. It is therefore always the front process in the queue that is next to have its delay expire. Processes can be added to the queue at any point.

8.4   Implementation of occam channels

The transputer's instruction set provides operations for inputting and outputting messages (it is also possible to enable an input when it forms part of an ALT guard). There is, necessarily, a clear distinction between the implementation of internal channels (within a single transputer) and external ones that must be mapped onto links. Essentially, the address of the channel enables this distinction to be apparent to the processor executing the I/O operations. Within this section the implementation of 'internal' and 'external' channels will be considered separately.

8.4.1   Internal channels

When a channel is defined a single word of storage is allocated. This memory location is loaded with a value that is distinct from any process id. Let that value be represented by the word empty. Figure 8.3 illustrates this channel word and the workspaces of the two processes, P and Q, that use this channel.

As it is an internal channel and only one process can be executing at any instance on that transputer then either P or Q will want to communicate first (the direction of the communication at this point is irrelevant). Assume P gets to the communication first; it will find that the value in the

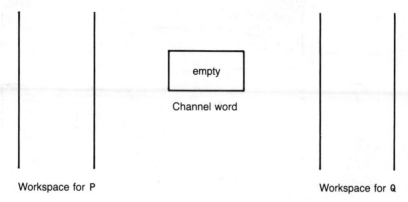

Figure 8.3 An empty channel.

channel word is empty, thus signifying that it is first and that it must wait. The actions it takes are as follows. It places, in the channel word, the id for process P (this will be a pointer into the workspace for P), see Figure 8.4. Then it stores the value of the next instruction register in its workspace, and finally it instructs the scheduler to run another process. P is now suspended; it is not executing and it is not in the queue of executable processes.

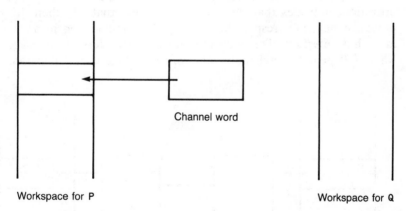

Figure 8.4 The first process arrives at the channel.

Eventually (presumably) process Q reaches the point at which it is ready to communicate with the channel. The channel word now does not contain empty and therefore Q knows that P is already waiting and a communication can take place, see Figure 8.5.

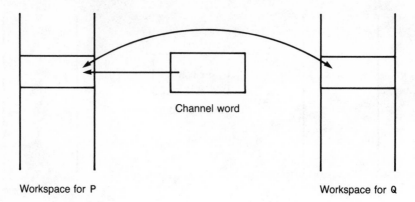

Workspace for P   Workspace for Q

Figure 8.5 The second process arrives at the channel.

The process Q has access to the id of P and can therefore initiate the transfer, regardless of the direction in which the transfer takes place. The message is copied (single object or block), P is added to the queue of executable processes and Q can continue. Note that Q was never suspended and that the message, whether it was a single item or a block transfer, passed directly between P and Q; it did not go 'through' the channel.

8.4.2 External channels

If the address of the named channel, in an input or output message operation, indicates that the channel is an external one then the main processor delegates responsibility for the communication to an autonomous link interface. This link interface both transfers the message and, when completed, reschedules the process. Figure 8.6 illustrates the

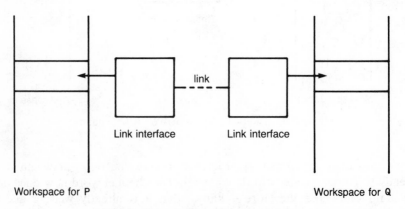

Workspace for P   Workspace for Q

Figure 8.6 A channel across a link.

structure of a communication between processes P and Q which are now executing on adjacent transputers. Both processes are suspended and the two link interfaces are exchanging data in the direction dictated by the program. The protocol used to transfer data is based on the serial transmission of byte values. It is therefore possible for two transputers of different word lengths to be connected by such a link.

Each link interface has three special registers, in which it stores, when activated, a pointer to the workspace of the process involved, a pointer to the message (source or destination) and a count of the number of bytes to be transferred. The link interface can store the message in the workspace, of the destination process, by DMA (Direct Memory Access) and can then add the suspended process to the queue of executable processes. Both of these actions take place without any direct interference with the main processor. Note, that due to processes not being allowed to share variables the use of DMA by the link interfaces is reliable. There cannot be any other active process wishing to use these memory locations. Indeed the only shared locations that need further protection are those dealing with the dispatch queues.

As a result of this autonomy a single transputer can, effectively, be processing and communicating at the same time. Indeed it is estimated that, in the extreme case, if all four links were transferring data in both directions then the maximum downgrade in the performance of the processor would be about 8%. (This assumes that all executing processes were at the same priority.) In the average situation the interference will be negligible.

This is a particularly significant point. Most analysis undertaken on multiprocessor systems assumes that each processor, at any instant, must either be communicating or processing, but not both. The architecture of the transputer gives considerable extra computer power over these systems.

8.5   Program distribution and start-up

The mapping of a channel onto an external link is expressed, within the occam program, by 'placing' both ends of the channel at appropriate addresses. This is done in conjunction with the use of a PLACE PAR constructor (see Chapter 3). Consider for example the following program outline:

```
CHAN OF INT Pipe:
PAR
   WHILE TRUE
     SEQ
       -- some actions including
       Pipe ! X -- for some data value X
```

```
WHILE TRUE
  SEQ
    Pipe ? Y
    -- other actions
```

The program consists of two main concurrent processes and they communicate via a single channel called Pipe. If the decision is made to execute these two processes on different (but linked) transputers then the code becomes:

```
CHAN OF INT Pipe:
PLACE PAR
  PROCESSOR 0
    PLACE Pipe AT Link0:
    WHILE TRUE
      SEQ
        -- some actions
        Pipe ! X
  PROCESSOR 1
    PLACE Pipe AT Link2:
    WHILE TRUE
      SEQ
        Pipe ? Y
        -- actions
```

The channel Pipe is allocated within each process, with the constants used (Link0 and Link2) being declared elsewhere to have the appropriate values. Figure 8.7 illustrates this structure (the second link on transputer 1 is physically joined to the zero link on transputer 0).

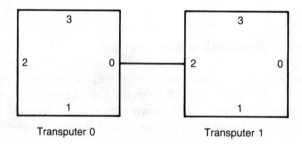

Figure 8.7 Two linked transputers.

This example can be expanded to illustrate the use of a replicator with a PLACED PAR. Figure 8.8 shows a pipeline of processes all of which are generated from the same PROC (process).

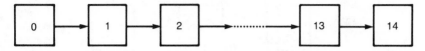

Figure 8.8 A pipeline of processes.

The occam code for this pipeline is:

```
[16]CHAN OF INT pipe:
PAR i = 0 FOR 15
  process(pipe[i],pipe[i + 1])
```

If this is to be mapped onto a series of connected transputers (numbered 0, 1,...,14) the code would have to be changed to the following:

```
[16]CHAN OF INT pipe:
PLACED PAR i = 0 FOR 15
  PROCESSOR i
    PLACE pipe[i] AT LINK0:
    PLACE pipe[i + 1] AT LINK3:
    process(pipe[i],pipe[i + 1])
```

One of the difficulties with multiprocessor systems is to distribute the software to the correct destination and to coordinate the powering up of all of the system's components. A single transputer, following power up, can be configured to bootstrap in either of two ways:

- Program available in ROM contained in the transputer's address space, or
- Program obtained down one of the serial links.

If the latter method is chosen then the first data to appear down any link will be taken to be code which, when loading is complete, will be executed. The other three links will be ignored until the program itself wishes to communicate with them.

An occam program is compiled on a host processor and then distributed to the target (the multi-transputer system) usually down a single link. The host processor, which could actually be a multi-transputer system itself, has an internal graph representing the topology of the target. It can therefore calculate the route by which the modules of code can reach the correct destinations. For example Figure 8.9 illustrates how a 3 × 3 matrix of transputers (without wrapped around links) could receive their programs if the host is connected to one of the corner transputers.

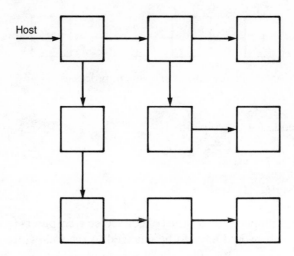

Figure 8.9   The initialization of a process matrix.

If each transputer is loaded with different modules then they must store their own code and then forward the subsequent modules down the appropriate links. Alternatively if the modules are generated from a PAR replicator, which will often be the case, then it is not necessary for the host to generate many copies of the code. Each transputer can be instructed to forward a copy of its own module.

With complex and large topologies care must be taken at start-up to ensure that a transputer does not receive data, from an initialized and executing neighbour, before it receives the program to deal with that data. If this eventuality were allowed to arise then the transputer would attempt to execute the data!

8.6   Summary

The above discussions have illustrated the close association between the occam language and the transputer. This modern fast processor provides registers for manipulating concurrent processes and instructions that can be easily generated by a compiler. Communication between processes is undertaken simply and efficiently whether or not the processes are on the same transputer. The result of these provisions is a truly flexible and versatile system. Not only can the number and topology of the processors be changed easily but the software can be distributed to these various structures with the minimum of disturbance. This can, however, only be done if the software itself was written (or transposed – see Chapter 10) to have significant parallelism within it.

The distribution of sequential programs to multiprocessor systems is non-trivial and usually leads to poor return on the investment of extra processors. Moreover the rewriting of programs to match new processor structures is itself error prone and costly. An occam program can be distributed to a collection of transputers without affecting the logical behaviour of the program, but only if sufficient concurrency was expressed in the program in the first place. The transputer supports an efficient implementation of concurrency even on a single transputer system; this allows programs, from the outset, to be designed with maximum concurrency.

The occam programmer should think of processes and synchronizations, not sequences of statements. As all actions in occam are undertaken by processes it is the PAR construct that is the more natural. The SEQ is a restricted form that imposes a sequential synchronization on the specified processes; it should only be used when the algorithm being implemented requires it. If an occam program is designed with considerations of concurrency paramount then the execution of that program on a single transputer, a pipeline or array of transputers, a tree structure or an arbitrary topology of transputers should be feasible.

This argument is equally valid for other processors as well as the transputer.

CHAPTER 9

Input and Output in Occam

As is usual with a modern high level language, input and output are not considered to be primary features in occam. Instead a method of defining implementation dependent high level I/O is provided. In addition facilities for managing low level I/O are supported. This chapter considers both of these approaches.

9.1 High level input and output

The basic model for I/O in occam is for channels to pass data between the program and the program's environment. A typical program will therefore have many internal channels and a few external ones. The external channels will be half in the program and half outside. Such channels are specified by explicitly allocating the channel:

```
allocation = PLACE name AT expression:

process = allocation
             process
```

An example of the allocation of a channel is:

```
CHAN OF P Fred:
PLACE Fred AT X:
```

where X is an implementation dependent constant; P is any protocol. On some of the occam development systems the value 1 indicated the VDU screen and 2 the keyboard. A simple program to echo characters is therefore:

```
CHAN OF ANY Screen:
PLACE Screen AT 1:
CHAN OF INT Keyboard:
PLACE Keyboard AT 2:
```

```
INT char:
WHILE TRUE
  SEQ
    Keyboard ? char
    Screen ! char
```

Note that although this program echoes characters, the internal data type is an INT (i.e. the ASCII representation of the character). As was indicated earlier the names Screen and Keyboard are not significant.

Other channel addresses can be used to interact with files and peripheral devices. If an implementation supports such facilities then there will be addresses defined. A more useful interface to a program's environment, however, would be achieved if standard library PROCs were available that had the appropriate channel definitions hidden. Such library PROCs are provided with the transputer development system (TDS).

9.2   Low level input and output

In order to construct device drivers for external entities a language must provide:

1. Facilities for interacting directly with control registers.
2. Facilities for handling interrupts.

As the transputer does not provide special instructions for controlling external devices, occam will only cater for (the more common) memory mapped I/O. It is possible to mix transputer assembler and occam to code unusual external devices but this provision is beyond the scope of this book. Moreover, many devices can be catered for in occam without recourse to this technique. An example is given below. It should also be noted at this point that it is acceptable to write PROCs in other high level languages; for example the transputer implementation of occam can support C, Pascal and FORTRAN77. I/O routines could therefore be programmed in another language entirely.

With memory mapped I/O the registers that form the interface between the main processor and the device are deemed to be located at specific addresses within the processor's memory space. To enable an occam program to use such registers they must also be in the program's address space. The registers themselves are used to give instructions to the device and to receive, or transmit, data. As an example consider a common analogue to digital converter (ADC). The converter samples some environmental factors such as temperature, it translates the measurements it receives and provides scaled integer values on a register. One such converter has a 16-bit control register with the following structure:

Bit	Name	Meaning
0	A/D Start	Set to 1 to start a conversion.
6	Interrupt Enable/Disable	Set to 1 to enable interrupts.
7	Done	Set to 1 when conversion is complete.
8–13	Channel	The converter has 64 analogue inputs, the particular one required is indicated by the value of the channel.
15	Error	Set to 1 by the converter if device malfunctions.

In order to read a particular analogue input a channel address (not to be confused with an occam channel) is given in bits 8 to 13 and then bit 0 is set to start the converter. When a value has been loaded into the results register the device will interrupt the processor. The error flag will then be checked before the results register is read. During this interaction it may be desirable to disable the interrupt.

To handle this device the control software must, therefore, have access to the results and control registers and be able to handle the interrupt. Such facilities are not usually found in a high level programming language but are available in Modula, Modula-2 and Ada (as well as occam).

When programming an embedded system in a concurrent programming language it is conceptually useful to extend the process model so that the external devices are considered to be 'hardware processes'. An entire system therefore consists of both hardware and software processes. It follows that the primitives used to give communication and synchronization between software processes should, if possible, also be used to give communication and synchronization between hardware and software processes.

As the occam model of interprocess communication is based on message passing, to the exclusion of shared variables, it is this style that is also applied to hardware processes. Registers are mapped on to **ports** that are conceptually similar to channels. For instance if a 16-bit register is at address X then a port is defined as:

```
PORT OF INT16 P:
PLACE P AT X:
```

Interaction with this register is obtained by reading or writing to this port:

```
P ! A  -- write value of A to the port

P ? B  -- read value of port into B
```

The distinction between ports and channel, which is a significant one, is that there is no synchronization associated with the port interaction. Neither reads nor writes can lead to the executing process being suspended; a value is always written to the address specified and, similarly, a value is always read. A port is thus a channel in which the partner is always ready to communicate (cf. TIMERS).

An interrupt is handled in occam as a rendezvous with the hardware processes. Associated with the interrupt there must be an implementation dependent address (Y); a channel is then mapped onto this address:

```
CHAN OF ANY Interrupt:
PLACE Interrupt AT Y:
```

The protocol for this channel will also be implementation dependent.

The interrupt handler will wait for an input from the designated channel:

```
INT Any:
SEQ
  -- using ports enable interrupt
  Interrupt ? Any
  -- actions necessary when interrupt has occurred.
```

The hardware interrupt handling mechanisms must therefore synchronize with the designated channel when an external interrupt occurs.

On the transputer the hardware interrupt will be connected to the EventIn pin, see Figure 8.1. This pin has a defined address within the processor; hence the interrupt channel is declared to be at that address. The mechanism surrounding the EventIn pin is such that if there is a process suspended on that address then that process will be made executable when an interrupt arrives.

To obtain responsiveness, the process handling the interrupt will usually be given a high priority. Therefore not only will it be made executable by the interrupt event but it will, within a short period of time, actually be executing (assuming that no other high priority process is running). On the transputer there is a defined upper bound on the real-time delay that will ensue before the process that handles the interrupt is actually doing so. Moreover once that high priority process is executing it cannot be removed from the processor unless it itself becomes suspended.

9.3   An example device driver

To illustrate the use of the low level I/O facilities that occam provides, a process will be developed that controls the analogue to digital converter described above. Traditionally this process is called a device driver.

A device driver will loop round receiving requests and providing results; it is programmed as a PROC with a two channel interface. When an address (for one of the 64 analogue input channels) is passed down input a 16-bit result will be returned via channel output. There are however further output states that must be represented; these extra states indicate error conditions. It follows that output must be defined to pass a variant protocol:

```
PROTOCOL Out
  CASE
    Correct ; INT16  -- correct output
    RangeError       -- input out of range
    AdcError         -- error flag set in ADC
    AdcOffLine       -- ADC does not respond
  :
CHAN OF INT16 request:
CHAN OF Out return:
PROC ADC(CHAN OF INT16 input, CHAN OF Out output)
  -- body of PROC, see below
PRI PAR
  ADC(request,return)
  PAR
    -- rest of program
```

A PRI PAR is desirable as the ADC must handle an interrupt each time it is used. Note, that three of the four variants do not have a data value associated with them, they consist only of the tag field.

Within the body of the PROC the interrupt channel (EventIn channel) and the two PORTs must first be declared:

```
PORT OF INT16 Control.Register:
PLACE Control.Register AT #AA12:
PORT OF INT16 Buffer.Register:
PLACE Buffer.Register AT #AA14:
CHAN OF ANY Interrupt:
PLACE Interrupt AT Event.In:
INT16 Control.R:  -- variable representing control buffer
```

Where #AA12 and #AA14 are the defined addresses for the two registers (in hex).

To instruct the hardware to undertake an operation requires bits 0 and 6 to be set on the control register; at the same time all other bits apart from those between 8 and 13 (inclusive) must be set to zero. This is achieved by using the following constants;

```
VAL INT16 zero IS 0:
VAL INT16 Go IS 65:
```

Having received an address from channel input its value must be assigned to bits 8 through 13 in the control register. This is accomplished by using a shift operation. The actions that must be taken in order to start a conversion are therefore:

```
INT16 Address:
SEQ
  input ? Address
  IF
    (Address < 0) OR (Address > 63)
      output ! RangeError  -- error condition
    TRUE
      SEQ
        Control.R := zero
        Control.R := Address << 8
        Control.R := Control.R \/ Go
        Control.Register ! Control.R
```

Once an interrupt has arrived the control register is read and the error flag and done checked. To do this the control register must be masking against appropriate constants:

```
VAL INT16 Done IS 128:
VAL INT16 Error IS MOSTNEG INT16:
```

MOSTNEG has the representation 1000000000000000.
    The checks are thus:

```
IF
  ((Done /\ Control.R) \/ (Error /\ Control.R)) <> zero
    -- error
  TRUE
    -- appropriate value is in buffer register
```

The device driver is structured so that three attempts are made to get a correct reading before passing the off-line error condition back to the requesting process.
    The code for the PROC can now be given:

```
PROC ADC(CHAN OF INT16 input, CHAN OF Out output)
  PORT OF INT16 Control.Register:
  PLACE Control.Register AT #AA12:
  PORT OF INT16 Buffer.Register:
  PLACE Buffer.Register AT #AA14:
  CHAN OF ANY Interrupt:
  PLACE Interrupt AT Event.In:
  TIMER CLOCK:
  INT16 Control.R:  -- variable representing control buffer
```

```
INT16 Buffer.R:   -- variable representing results buffer
INT Time:
VAL INT16 zero IS 0:
VAL INT16 Go IS 65:
VAL INT16 Done IS 128:
VAL INT16 Error IS MOSTNEG INT16:
VAL INT Timeout IS 600000: -- or some other appropriate value
INT Any:
INT16 Address,i:
BOOL Found,Error:
WHILE TRUE
  SEQ
    input ? Address
    IF
      (Address < 0) OR (Address > 63)
        output ! RangeError -- error condition
      TRUE
        SEQ
          i := 1
          Error := FALSE
          Found := FALSE
          WHILE (i < 3) AND ((NOT Found) AND (NOT Error))
            -- Three attempts are made to get a reading from
            -- the ADC. This reading may be either correct or
            -- is flagged as being an error.
            SEQ
              Control.R := zero
              Control.R := Address << 8
              Control.R := Control.R \/ Go
              Control.Register ! Control.R
              CLOCK ? Time
              ALT
                Interrupt ? Any
                  SEQ
                    Control.Register ? Control.R
                    IF
                      (Done /\ Control.R) \/ (Error /\ Control.R) <> zero
                        SEQ
                          Error := TRUE
                          output ! AdcError -- error condition
                      TRUE
                        SEQ
                          Found := TRUE
                          Buffer.Register ? Buffer.R
                          output ! Correct ; Buffer.R
                CLOCK ? AFTER Time PLUS Timeout
                  -- The device is not responding
                  i := i + 1
          IF
```

```
(NOT Found) AND (NOT Error)
  output ! AdcOffLine
TRUE
  SKIP
```
:

In this code although the device driver is running at a high priority the client process is not and hence the driver will be delayed until the client can read from `return` (which is mapped on to the `CHAN` parameter `output`). With input devices that generate data asynchronously this delay could lead to the driver missing an interrupt. To overcome this the input data must be buffered. A suitable circular buffer was illustrated in Section 3.6.2 and Figure 3.6. Remember that because the `ALT` in the buffer cannot have output guards another single buffer item is needed.

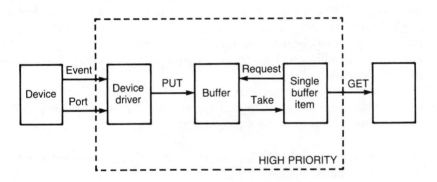

Figure 9.1   A real-time device driver.

To ensure that the device driver is not delayed by the scheduling algorithm for the low priority client process the two buffer processes (as well as the driver) must execute at high priority. This is illustrated in Figure 9.1.

CHAPTER 10

Transforming Occam Programs

One of the attractive features of the occam programming language is that its semantics can be formally stated. Although such a description is beyond the scope of this book a denotation semantics for occam (an earlier version) can be found in Roscoe (1985). The availability of such an analysis makes it possible formally to specify and verify occam programs. In particular the ability to prove that a program is deadlock free would have obvious benefits.

Another use of formal techniques is in the transformation of one occam program into another that is, in some sense, equivalent. The motivations for transforming a program are:

- To change a clear but inefficient program into an efficient but perhaps obscure one.
- To change a sequential program into a concurrent program to exploit parallel hardware.
- To change a concurrent program into a sequential one for more efficient execution on a single processor.
- To change a physically infeasible program into a physically feasible one.

The latter transformation may be needed to map a program onto a transputer system where there are only four links available for communication between distributed sections of the code.

Informally a transformation can be said to change the structure of a program without changing its meaning. This does not, however, imply that the behaviour of the transformed program and its original will be identical; in particular the speeds at which they execute will differ (this being one of the objectives in performing the transformation).

To perform a single complex transformation to a sizeable program in a way that guarantees that the program will not become invalid is far from being a trivial undertaking. Rather it is better to apply a series of simple transformations each of which clearly leaves the program essentially the same as before. These simple transformations can be expressed as 'laws'; although the name is perhaps misleading. Example laws are illustrated below. A complete and formal description of these laws can be found in Roscoe and Hoare (1986). Even if one is not concerned with trans-formation techniques, these laws are useful in re-emphasizing some of the important properties of the language components.

10.1   Laws of occam

The analysis of occam programs is made much easier if the programs are assumed to be canonical; that is, there are no variable names re-used. This can always be achieved by substitution, or formally, within occam, by abbreviations (see Chapter 6).

To simplify the presentation of occam syntax, brackets will be used; for example, rather than:

```
SEQ
  A
  B
  C
```

we will write, for this chapter only,

```
SEQ (A,B,C)
```

Where a construct is considered to have an arbitrary number of com-ponents (i.e. n) it is written as follows:

$$\underset{i=1}{\overset{n}{\text{PAR}}} \text{Pi} \qquad \underset{i=1}{\overset{n}{\text{SEQ}}} \text{Si} \qquad \underset{i=1}{\overset{n}{\text{ALT}}} \text{gipi} \qquad \underset{i=1}{\overset{n}{\text{IF}}} \text{bipi}$$

Two simple equivalence rules can now be stated (they are numbered for later reference):

```
SEQ ( ) = SKIP                                                    (1)
PAR ( ) = SKIP                                                    (2)
```

The equality symbol implies that the program fragment on the right is equivalent to, or essentially the same as, the fragment on the left. For most laws equality also implies symmetry (i.e. the left is also equivalent to the right) but this is not always the case.

Laws (1) and (2) merely state that an empty sequence (or PAR block) is equivalent to SKIP.

10.1.1   Associativity

It was noted in Chapter 3 that both the SEQ and PAR constructs are associative:

```
SEQ(P,Q,R) = SEQ(P,SEQ(Q,R))                                    (3)
PAR(P,Q,R) = PAR(P,PAR(Q,R))                                    (4)
```

where P,Q and R are arbitrary processes.

Nested IFs and ALTs are also associate:

```
IF(C1,IF(C2),C3) = IF(C1,C2,C3)                                 (5)
ALT(G1,ALT(G2),G3) = ALT(G1,G2,G3)                             (6)
```

where C is a collection of (b,p), Boolean expressions and subprocesses; and G is a collection of (g,p), guards and subprocesses. If an IF process does not contain a Boolean expression then it is impossible for any of the Boolean expressions to evaluate TRUE. Similarly, if there are no guards in an ALT none can be ready. It follows that:

```
IF( ) = STOP                                                    (7)
ALT( ) = STOP                                                   (8)
```

Law (5) applies to one form of nesting IF constructors where the inner IF is in place of the usual (b,p). Another form of nesting is derived if an inner IF is one of the p subprocesses. Again it is possible to remove the nesting:

```
IF(C, b1, IF(b2,p)) = IF(C, IF(b1 AND b2, p))                  (9)
```

Law (9) is only valid if the inner IF is the last subprocess; alternatively it is valid in any position if the inner IF is **complete**. A complete IF constructor is one that is guaranteed to have a Boolean expression that evaluates TRUE. Any IF process can be made complete by adding at the end:

```
TRUE
  STOP
```

All that this addition does is make the STOP condition explicit, rather than have it implied implicitly by the semantics of the IF.

In the general case the inner IF will contain more than one (b,p) component. To illustrate the use of laws (5) and (9) consider the following code:

```
IF
  A > 0
    IF I = 1 FOR 3
      B[I] > 0
        ch ! A         -- for some channel ch
```

```
TRUE
  ch ! 0
```

The replicator is merely a shorthand notation and can be expanded:

```
IF
  A > 0
    IF
      B[1] > 0
        ch ! A
      B[2] > 0
        ch ! A
      B[3] > 0
        ch ! A
  TRUE
    ch ! 0
```

In this form the inner IF is neither complete nor the last subprocess; in order to apply law (9) it must first be made complete:

```
IF
  A > 0
    IF
      B[1] > 0
        ch ! A
      B[2] > 0
        ch ! A
      B[3] > 0
        ch ! A
      TRUE
        STOP
  TRUE
    ch ! 0
```

Law (9) can now remove the first level of nesting:

```
IF
  IF
    A > 0 AND B[1] > 0
      ch ! A
    A > 0 AND B[2] > 0
      ch ! A
    A > 0 AND B[3] > 0
      ch ! A
    A > 0 AND TRUE
      STOP
  TRUE
    ch ! 0
```

The second level of nesting is removed by applying law (5) to give:

```
IF
  A > 0 AND B[1] > 0
    ch ! A
  A > 0 AND B[2] > 0
    ch ! A
  A > 0 AND B[3] > 0
    ch ! A
  A > 0
    STOP
  TRUE
    ch ! 0
```

In the above the Boolean expression before the STOP has been reduced by removing the superfluous AND TRUE.

10.1.2 Symmetry

A number of constructs within occam are not dependent upon the order in which their subcomponents are expressed. The most obvious example of this is the PAR:

$$\text{PAR}_{i=1}^{n} \text{Pi} = \text{PAR}_{i=1}^{n} \text{P}\Pi(i) \tag{10}$$

where Π is any permutation of the values $\{1, 2, ..., n\}$. A PAR process with n subprocesses can therefore have these subprocesses rearranged, arbitrarily. It is said to be symmetric. The same applies to the ALT:

$$\text{ALT}_{i=1}^{n} \text{Gi} = \text{ALT}_{i=1}^{n} \text{G}\Pi(i) \tag{11}$$

The standard IF processes cannot be rearranged as it is the first TRUE Boolean expression that determines which subprocess is executed. However if the Boolean expressions are pairwise disjoint then a permutation is possible. The Boolean expressions are said to be pairwise disjoint if only one can be TRUE for any set of values for the associated variables. For example the following IF has this property:

```
IF
  X > 0
    Y := 1
  X = 0
    Y := 0
```

```
X < 0
   Y := -1
```

The following law thus applies to the IF:

$$
\begin{array}{ll}
\text{n} & \text{n} \\
\text{IF bi,pi} = \text{IF bII(i),pII(i)} \\
\text{i = 1} & \text{i = 1}
\end{array}
\tag{12}
$$

provided that bi AND bj = TRUE implies i = j.

10.1.3   Replacing SEQ by PAR

One obvious means of increasing the parallelism in an occam program is to replace, where allowed and where useful, a SEQ construct by a PAR:

$$
\text{SEQ(P,R)} = \text{PAR(P,R)}
\tag{13}
$$

This equivalence is correct provided the set of variables (and channels) used in P and R are disjoint. This rule is, in fact, slightly stronger than that required, for if P and R both read a common variable then the replacement can still take place.

Perhaps the simplest transformation between a SEQ and a PAR comes from the equivalence of the basic channel operations:

```
PAR
   C ! X
   C ? Y
```

and the assignment:

```
Y := X
```

This can be represented as a law as follows:

$$
\text{PAR(C ! X,C ? Y)} = \text{Y := X}
\tag{14}
$$

Another form of this law is obtained if a simple assignment is replaced by an assignment through a channel:

```
SEQ(P,x := y,Q) =
   CHAN OF PRO Z:
   PAR(SEQ(P,Z ! y),SEQ(Z ? x,Q))
```
(15)

where y is a variable of P (only) and x is a variable of Q (only). P and Q have no variables in common. PRO is the appropriate protocol.

The new channel introduced, Z, must have a distinct name. For example the code:

```
SEQ
  ch1 ? A
  GetX(A,X)
  Y := X / 2.0
  GetZ(Y,Z)
  ch2 ! Z
```

where GetX is a procedure call that evaluates X when given A and GetZ does similar with Y and Z; could be changed to:

```
-- definition of new channel New.Chan
PAR
  SEQ
    ch1 ? A
    GetX(A,X)
    New.Chan ! X / 2.0
  SEQ
    New.Chan ? Y
    GetZ(Y,Z)
    ch2 ! Z
```

This rule enables a sequence of processes that can be split into two distinct parts, that are only linked by an assignment statement, to be transformed into two parallel processes linked via a channel.

10.1.4 Laws of declaration

Not only are there laws to govern the transformation of one construct into another but there are others that deal with declarations. For example declarations are associative:

$$T\ a:\ (T\ b:\ P) = T\ a,b:\ P \tag{16}$$

where P is some process and T is any valid type.
Declarations can also be eliminated if they are not used:

$$T\ a:\ P = P \tag{17}$$

if a is not used in P.
It is useful if declarations that are embedded within a program can be moved to the beginning of the program. This can be achieved by applying a series of laws that link declarations and the program constructs. There are two that involve SEQ:

$$SEQ(T\ a:\ P,Q) = T\ a:\ SEQ(P,Q) \tag{18}$$

provided a is not used in Q; and

    SEQ(P,T a: Q) = T a: SEQ(P,Q)   (19)

provided a is not used in P.

Other laws exist that apply to ALTs, IFs and PARs.

10.1.5 Rearranging a loop

Many programs in occam take the form of a pipeline of processes with each element in the pipeline being linked to its neighbours by a single channel, see Figure 10.1. Within each process a sequence of actions is repeated indefinitely:

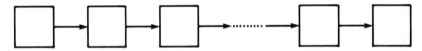

Figure 10.1 A general pipeline of processes.

```
WHILE TRUE
  SEQ
    in ? X
    -- process X to produce Y
    out ! Y
```

where X is compatible with the protocol of channel in, and Y is compatible with out.

The code is entirely sequential even though the two channel actions are independent. To increase the parallelism in this code the loop must first be rearranged; in the following let W stand for WHILE TRUE:

    W(SEQ(P,Q,R)) = SEQ(P,W(SEQ(Q,R,P)))   (20)

If R and P are independent then SEQ(Q,R,P) can be replaced by SEQ(Q,PAR(R,P)). This could not have been done before applying law (20) as R and P did not appear together.

To illustrate this law consider the following simple processing

```
WHILE TRUE
  SEQ
    in ? X
    Y := X * X
    out ! Y
```

Applying law (20) transforms this to:

```
SEQ
  in ? X
  WHILE TRUE
    SEQ
      Y := X * X
      out ! Y
      in ? X
```

Law (13) now can be applied to the final two processes:

```
SEQ
  in ? X
  WHILE TRUE
    SEQ
      Y := X * X
      PAR
        out ! Y
        in ? X
```

The result of performing these two transformations is to have a program in which the two actions that can lead to delay are expressed as being concurrent. A delay at one point in the pipeline will not therefore immediately delay the entire pipeline.

10.1.6 Unravelling a replicated SEQ

Law (20) which applies to a WHILE loop can also be used, in a slightly different form, to reorder a replicated SEQ. Let:

```
SEQ i = 1 FOR n
  SEQ
    P(i)
    Q(i)
```

be represented by:

$$\text{SEQ}(Pi,Qi) \quad i = 1 \ldots n$$

$$\sideset{}{}{\mathop{\text{SEQ}}_{i=1}^{n}}(Pi,Qi)$$

then:

$$\mathop{\text{SEQ}}_{i=1}^{n}(Pi,Qi) = \mathop{\text{SEQ}}_{i=1}^{n-1}(P1,\text{SEQ}(Qi,Pi + 1),Qn) \tag{21}$$

If Qi and Pi + 1 are independent then a PAR could also be introduced. The following example illustrates how law (21) could be applied:

```
SEQ i = 1 FOR 16
  SEQ
    A[i] := C[i] + i
    B[i] := A[i] + B[i]
```

This becomes:

```
SEQ
  A[1] := C[1] + 1
  SEQ i = 1 FOR 15
    SEQ
      B[i] := A[i] + B[i]
      A[i + 1] := C[i + 1]+(i + 1)
  B[16] := A[16] + B[16]
```

10.1.7 Distributivity

PAR and SEQ can be related by a law that can be seen as a form of distributivity:

```
PAR(SEQ(A,B),SEQ(C,D))
  = SEQ(PAR(A,C),PAR(B,D))                              (22)
```

Note that the necessary conditions implied by the left hand fragment (namely B must follow A; D must follow C; A is independent of C & D; and B is independent of C & D) are all satisfied by the right hand side. For example:

```
PAR
  SEQ
    ch1 ? A
    B := A * 16
  SEQ
    ch2 ? C
    D := C * 16
```

is equivalent to:

```
SEQ
  PAR
    ch1 ? A
    ch2 ? C
  PAR
    B := A * 16
    D := C * 16
```

Consider another example:

```
PAR
  SEQ
    C ! X
    P1
  SEQ
    C ? Y
    P2
```

In this code P1 is some process that updates X, and P2 is a process that uses Y. By applying law (22) we obtain

```
SEQ
  PAR
    C ! X
    C ? Y
  PAR
    P1
    P2
```

If we then apply law (14) this reduces to

```
SEQ
  Y := X
  PAR
    P1
    P2
```

10.1.8 Summary

In the above section a number of laws have been introduced that allow transformations to be applied, reliably, to small sections of occam code. Many of the laws are, in themselves, obvious and, perhaps, trivial. But together they represent a powerful set of techniques. Moreover, unlike compiler optimization techniques, they apply to program source and yield valid language forms. The laws themselves can be formally specified which makes it possible for some of the transformations to be undertaken by appropriate software tools.

Moreover, these laws are not only useful in transforming individual programs but they can be employed to test whether two programs are actually equivalent. This is done by transforming both programs to what is known as a **normal form**. A normal form for finite occam programs is described by Roscoe and Hoare (1986).

To illustrate how a combination of transformations can be applied, an example of matrix multiplication will be given. This example will be expressed in terms of a systolic action and is an adaptation of analysis given by May and Taylor (1984).

10.2   An example of a systolic algorithm

One of the reasons for having concurrency within the programming language is to be able to represent (and ultimately implement) algorithms that are destined for parallel execution. A systolic algorithm is one that has a collection (often a matrix) of identical processes through which data flows. The term systolic is used as there is an analogy here with blood flowing around the human body. In a 'pure' systolic algorithm each of the parallel processes executes an identical sequence of instructions. They can therefore be implemented on SIMD (Single Instruction Multiple Data) architectures. More flexibility is nevertheless possible if the actual instructions executed are dependent upon the data flowing through.

A system of transputers is ideally suited to this form of algorithm; each transputer can hold a process (generated from a single PROC) and the data can flow down the links. Although each transputer is running the same process, in the sense that they have all been generated from the same PROC, the code may contain IF processes, for example, which will mean that different instructions are being executed on different transputers.

One example of a systolic algorithm is the multiplication of two matrices where each node of the resulting matrix is represented by a single process. Two $M \times M$ square matrices (A and B) are multiplied as follows:

$$R = A * B$$

where any particular element of R is calculated as a sum of a series of length M:

$$r(i, j) = \sum_{k=1}^{M} a(i, k)* b(k, j)$$

For example:

$$
\begin{aligned}
r(4, 5) = \quad & a(4, 1) * b(1, 5) \\
+ \; & a(4, 2) * b(2, 5) \\
+ \; & ... \\
+ \; & a(4, M) * b(M, 5)
\end{aligned}
$$

A parallel multiplication algorithm maps each element of R onto a process. Each process receives a flow of values (representing matrices A and B) which it uses and then passes on. This is illustrated in Figure 10.2. The code for each process can therefore be generated from a single PROC.

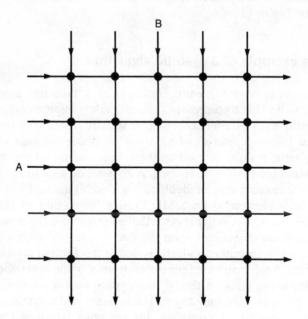

Figure 10.2   A process matrix.

```
PROC Mult(CHAN OF INT N,S,E,W)
  INT Result:
  INT A,B:
  SEQ
    Result := 0
    SEQ i = 0 FOR M
      SEQ
        PAR
          N ? A
          W ? B
        Result := Result + (A * B)
        PAR
          S ! A
          E ! B
  :
```

M pairs of values are read, Results is updated accordingly and the values are passed on.

For an M × M matrix, M * (M + 1) channels are required in the vertical and horizontal planes. A matrix of channels is thus required:

```
[M * (M + 1)]CHAN OF INT Vert,Horz:
```

The processes that generate the two matrices to be multiplied can be defined by two PROCs, GenerateA and GenerateB.

```
PROC GenerateA ([]CHAN OF INT Avalues)
PROC GenerateB ([]CHAN OF INT Bvalues)
```

The form these PROCs take is of little interest here; they are therefore not given. To multiply the two matrices requires the following harness program:

```
VAL M is 8 :
[M * (M + 1)]CHAN OF INT Vert,Horz:
PAR
  PAR i = 0 FOR M
    PAR j = 0 FOR M
      Mult(Vert[(M * i) + j],Vert[(M * i) +(j + 1)],
           Horz[(M * i) +j],Horz[(M * (i + 1)) + j])
```

10.3   Transforming the matrix example

The PROC given above for the Mult procedure consists, essentially, of a repeat of three actions; input new values, update the variable result, output the values. This is a sequential structure. The power of the systolic approach is in executing each instance of Mult in parallel. It is however possible to transform the code given for the PROC so that it is more parallel. In particular it would be useful to execute all four channel operations in parallel. Although for this simple example it may be obvious how to change the program, the objective of this discussion is not the particular example under investigation but to illustrate how a program may be changed by the systematic application of the laws discussed earlier in this chapter.

An examination of the Mult PROC shows that most of its execution is focused on the replicated SEQ:

```
SEQ i = 0 FOR M
  SEQ
    PAR
      N ? A
      W ? B
    Result := Result + (A * B)
    PAR
      S ! A
      E ! B
```

The last two elements of the SEQ are independent and can therefore be executed in parallel (law 13):

```
SEQ i = 0 FOR M
  SEQ
    PAR
      N ? A
      W ? B
    PAR
      Result := Result + (A * B)
      PAR
        S ! A
        E ! B
```

By the law of association (law 4) the final PAR can be removed; the last five lines of the above then become:

```
PAR
  Result := Result + (A * B)
  S ! A
  E ! B
```

The replicated SEQ now applies to two subprocesses and can therefore be unravelled by law (21):

```
SEQ
  PAR
    N ? A
    W ? B
  SEQ i = 0 FOR M - 1
    SEQ
      PAR
        Result := Result + (A * B)
        S ! A
        E ! B
      PAR
        N ? A
        W ? B
  PAR
    Result := Result + (A * B)
    S ! A
    E ! B
```

We now concentrate on the reads from N and W (inside the new replicated SEQ):

```
PAR
  N ? A
  W ? B
```

It is a trivial rule (not included above) that a channel read:

```
N ? A
```

is equivalent to:

```
INT Atemp:
SEQ
  N ? Atemp
  A := Atemp
```

for some new variable Atemp. The above PAR can therefore be transformed to:

```
PAR
  INT Atemp:
  SEQ
    N ? Atemp
    A := Atemp
  INT Btemp:
  SEQ
    W ? Btemp
    B := Btemp
```

The declarations can be moved by application of laws that are similar to (18) and (19):

```
INT Atemp,Btemp:
PAR
  SEQ
    N ? Atemp
    A := Atemp
  SEQ
    W ? Btemp
    B := Btemp
```

By law (22) this PAR(SEQ,SEQ) can be changed to a SEQ(PAR,PAR):

```
INT Atemp,Btemp:
SEQ
  PAR
    N ? Atemp
    W ? Btemp
  PAR
    A := Atemp
    B := Btemp
```

It is wasteful to do the two assignments in parallel; the last PAR can therefore be replaced by a SEQ (law 13). The law of association (law 3) can then be applied to yield:

```
INT Atemp,Btemp:
SEQ
  PAR
    N ? Atemp
    W ? Btemp
  A := Atemp
  B := Btemp
```

The replicated SEQ has now become (again the declaration of the temporary variables has been moved):

```
INT Atemp,Btemp:
SEQ i = 0 FOR M - 1
  SEQ                 -- Y
    PAR
      Result := Result + (A * B)
      S ! A
      E ! B
    PAR
      N ? Atemp
      W ? Btemp
    A := Atemp
    B := Btemp
```

We are, at last, at the point at which we can apply the last two transformations. The first two components of the SEQ marked by Y are independent and can therefore be replaced by a PAR (law 13). Moreover this PAR then has the form PAR(PAR,PAR); the inner PARs can hence be removed by the associativity rule (law 4) to give:

```
INT Atemp,Btemp:
SEQ i = 0 FOR M - 1
  SEQ
    PAR
      Result := Result + (A * B)
      S ! A
      E ! B
      N ? Attempt
      W ? Btemp
    A := Atemp
    B := Btemp
```

The PROC for Mult has thus been transferred to the following structure.

```
PROC Mult (CHAN OF INT N,S,E,W)
  INT A,B:
  INT Result:
  SEQ
    Result := 0
    PAR
      N ? A
      W ? B
    INT Atemp,Btemp:
    SEQ i = 0 FOR M - 1
      SEQ
        PAR
          Result := Result + (A * B)
          S ! A
          E ! B
          N ? Atemp
          W ? Btemp
        A := Atemp
        B := Btemp
    Result := Result + (A * B)
    PAR
      S ! A
      E ! B
:
```

All the important actions associated with this procedure (the four channel transfers) are now parallel. Each node in the matrix can read in new values concurrently with outputting old values.

Although the transformations applied above have generated many pages of description, the result is a new program that we can be assured is equivalent to the old. Nothing has been done that could have invalidated assertions applied to the original code. These techniques (although considerable research effort is still being applied to them) promise to be of considerable importance to the occam programmer.

1

~~am and Ada –
A Comparison

One of the most important developments over the last decade in computing has been the emergence of the Ada programming language. Many readers will no doubt be familiar with this language and will have noted that there are clear similarities between the features that occam supports and the tasking model of Ada. This chapter compares the two languages in terms of their basic structures and their models of concurrency. Some prior knowledge of Ada is necessarily assumed but no new material about occam is introduced.

The Ada language is defined by an ANSI standard (*Ada Reference Manual*, 1983) and many introductory books are available (for example Barnes, 1984). Its tasking facilities have been thoroughly investigated (Burns *et al.*, 1987) and there are various tutorial texts (Burns, 1985; Gehani, 1984).

11.1 Sequential language structures

Ada is a large language with Pascal-like control structures, and re-entrant procedures and functions. It was designed in response to requirements specified by the US Department of Defense (DoD), that were primarily concerned with the programming of embedded systems. Ada supports a range of scalar types (integers, Booleans, characters and floating point and fixed point reals), multidimensional arrays (with dynamic bounds) and records (with variant components). In addition it enables objects to be constructed dynamically by providing heap management facilities. It also allows programmers to create new types by either specifying all values objects of that type can take (enumeration types) or by deriving them from predefined types.

From even this brief description it should be clear that there is a much richer collection of data types in Ada than there is in occam.

One area where the designers of Ada have introduced some significant language features is in the support of 'programming in the large'. The **package** structure allows related objects to be encapsulated to form distinct modules within a program. These modules can be individually developed and separately compiled, and support the hierarchical development of programs. A package can be used to implement an abstract data type or to provide information hiding; it is the single most important feature of Ada. In addition to the package, Ada also enables **generic** modules to be constructed which act as templates from which actual packages (or procedures) can be generated. Generics are aimed at improving the re-usability of code.

Again it can be seen that the present version of occam does not provide comparable functionality. Although it was mentioned earlier that some occam programming support environments may allow PROCs to be separately compiled and syntax sensitive editors may enable a program to be viewed at different levels of detail.

Another relatively new language feature that is supported in Ada, though not in occam, is **exception handling**. In order to increase the reliability of Ada software it is possible to write code that will trap errors and enable remedial action to be taken. On a transputer system errors are broadcast by the StopProc pin that can be linked to the EventIn pin on another transputer. This mechanism could form the basis of an error recovery facility; however this is a transputer specific, rather than a general occam, solution.

11.2   Concurrent execution

In both Ada and occam the unit of parallelism is the conventional one of a sequential process. There is however a clear distinction between the level at which processes are introduced and used within the two languages. With Ada, the process, which is called a **task**, is a high level construct containing, usually, a significant number of sequential statements. In occam the notion of process is much more low level, all statements are considered to be processes.

A series of actions in Ada is expressed, conventionally, as a sequence of statements. In occam such a series is represented by a set of processes that are defined to execute in a given sequence. A simple change to an occam program redefines this set of processes to have a concurrent execution. The difference between a sequence of statements and a collection of tasks, in Ada, is fundamental. For example, consider the execution of two procedure calls (proc1 and proc2). The sequential form (in occam and Ada) is as follows:

```
SEQ        -- occam
  proc1
  proc2
```

```
begin        -- Ada
   proc1;
   proc2;
end;
```

In occam concurrent execution is expressed simply as:

```
PAR
   proc1
   proc2
```

To achieve concurrency in Ada requires the introduction of two tasks:

```
declare
   task one;
   task two;
   task body one is
   begin
      proc1;
   end one;
   task body two is
   begin
      proc2;
   end two;
begin
   null;
end;
```

The actions that the two tasks undertake are defined by the task bodies. Task one therefore executes a call to proc1 and task two similarly calls proc2. Both tasks start their concurrent executions prior to the main program executing the null statement.

It is possible to write an Ada program that contains no concurrency. A significant subset of Ada represents a powerful sequential programming language. The task object and the message passing mechanism are additions to this sequential model, although the interaction between the tasking and the non-tasking features is non-trivial. Occam cannot be described in this way; the concept of process is basic to the language.

An occam program is a hierarchy of processes; primitive processes are grouped together to form higher order processes and some, such as an instance of a non-trivial procedure, will have a complexity comparable with an Ada task. At the topmost level the complete occam program is viewed as a single process. Ada tasks are similarly hierarchical and the main program can be considered to be a task. This hierarchy cannot, however, be extended down to the primitive level.

11.2.1 Representation

Tasks in Ada are named and syntactically consist of two distinct parts; a specification and a body:

```
task example;

task body example is
  -- internal declarations
begin
  -- sequence of statements
end example;
```

Tasks are not parameterized; the only way to pass information to a newly created task is to communicate with it. The use of PROCs with arbitrary parameter lists to encapsulate a concurrent object is clearly more expressive.

A task may be declared at any program level and are created implicitly after entry to the scope of their declarations. An instance of a task can also be created directly by the action of the 'new' operator; thereby giving a structure that is fully dynamic. As was indicated earlier occam has a static structure.

11.2.2 Termination

Both Ada and occam allow a process to execute an infinite loop and thereby never terminate. This structure is often used in embedded systems. Natural termination, when all actions have been performed and all subprocesses have terminated, can be observed in both languages. In addition to this 'normal' case an Ada task can terminate if:

1. an exception is raised but not handled (or handled only at the outer level); or
2. a terminate alternative on a select statement (see below) is executed when the parent of the task wishes to terminate and all subtasks of that parent have either terminated or are similarly waiting on terminate alternatives; or
3. it is aborted.

Occam does not provide an abort facility or a terminate alternative. If an error occurs then that process becomes equivalent to the primitive process STOP. It follows that a wayward process, or a collection of deadlocked processes, cannot be forcibly terminated. However, the existence of an abort facility is one of the more controversial features of Ada. Its inclusion reflects the need to be able to remove wayward tasks and yet its presence within the language is itself a source of unreliability (see 11.4).

11.3   Synchronization and communication

Tasks in Ada may communicate through any variable that is in scope. The responsibility for providing mutual exclusion over the use of such variables is the user's. This structure is further complicated by considerations of implementation which allows, for optimization purposes, copies of shared variables to be kept in each task's memory space. These copies are updated at defined synchronization points that lead to rules being required to govern the use of such variables between synchronization points. A compiler is not required, by the language definition, to recognize when these rules are broken. The program is, nevertheless, deemed to be 'erroneous'.

Shared variables are not meant to be the primary means of communication in Ada. The facility is included because 'to disallow shared variables seems to be a constraint which would be unwise in certain critical circumstances' (Ichbiah *et al.*, 1979). However as Welsh and Lister (1981) commented 'to allow them is equally unwise in others'.

Occam's association with the transputer has meant that from the outset it has used a model of concurrency that precludes shared variables. Its development from CSP and the requirement for a usable formal model of the language has also mitigated against the use of shared objects.

It follows therefore that Ada and occam both base their communication and synchronization on message passing. There are however important differences between the two models that the languages implement; these differences will be discussed below.

11.3.1   Process naming

Occam processes are not named, it is therefore necessary during communication to use indirect naming. This indirect naming is symmetric.

All normal tasks in Ada are named; the only exception to this are 'anonymous' tasks with which communication is only possible using shared memory. Ada uses direct, asymmetric naming:

```
T.E(X);   -- pass the value contained in variable X
          -- to the entry E in task T
accept E (V : in <some type>) do  -- read from any calling
                                  -- task into variable Y the
    Y := V;                       -- value given on the entry call
end E;
```

Entries within Ada tasks are defined within the task specification:

```
task T is
  entry E (V : in <some type>);
  -- other entries
end T;
```

Asymmetric naming in Ada supports the use of the client/server paradigm. Servers can be designed, coded and tested without knowledge of the exact client population; this cannot be done directly in occam. However, as a result of this Ada structure any entry may have a queue of calls outstanding. This queue (which is handled in a FIFO manner) presents an overhead to the run-time system. As occam channels are one-to-one there can be at most only a single request waiting, hence no queue mechanisms are required.

11.3.2   Synchronization model

Occam implements a standard rendezvous; a channel can only be used in one direction and we therefore have synchronous message passing. Ada provides an extended rendezvous with data passing in both directions (if required). The model is remote invocation (Burns *et al.*, 1987):

```
accept E (X : in Xtype; Y : out Ytype) do
  -- use X
  -- construct Y
end E;
```

Note that, not only is data passing in both directions but processing is being carried out during the rendezvous. There is thus the possibility of an error manifesting itself while the rendezvous is being executed. For example, the execution of an infinite loop will prohibit the rendezvous from termination. If an exception is raised, but not handled, within a rendezvous then the exception is propagated to both partners in the communication.

11.3.3   Message structure

Ada uses the same parameter passing model for entry calls as it does for procedure calls. Any number of objects may be passed and each can have any legal structure including predefined and user defined types; variant records, linked lists and multidimensional arrays. Occam now allows arbitrary collections of objects to be communicated within a single block transfer. However, Ada still has a more extensive collection of data structures to use during communication and processing.

11.3.4   Selective waiting

With any concurrent programming language basing its interprocess communication facilities on synchronous message passing, or remote invocation, there is a need to allow a process to wait for one of a number of possible communications. To this end Ada provides the select statement which can be compared with the occam ALT process. For example the following program segments both allow a process to wait for one of two integer communications:

```
select
  accept C1 (I : integer) do
    value := I;
  end C1;
or
  accept C2 (I : integer) do
    value := I;
  end C2;
end select;

ALT
  C1 ? value     -- value is of type INT
    SKIP
  C2 ? value
    SKIP
```

If there are outstanding calls on two or more branches of the construct then neither language defines which call is to be accepted. The algorithm is said to be arbitrary. There is, however, a terminology difference between the two constructs in respect of the concept of guard. Both languages use a Boolean expression to 'close off' or avoid certain actions. However, in Ada a guard is only this Boolean expression:

```
select
  when <Boolean expression> =>     -- guard
    accept E( ... ) do
      <action>
    end E;
```

In occam the term 'guard' refers to the more conventional structure which includes the Boolean expression and the channel communication.

Only receive messages are allowed with the standard Ada select and the occam ALT. The expressive power of Ada is however increased by allowing data to pass in either or both directions. An occam guard can only contain an input operation.

11.3.5 Timeouts

Both languages allow a process to express a timeout on a receive operation. In Ada the delay is given relative to current time; occam uses absolute time and therefore the present value of the local real-time clock must be accessed. To obtain a value of the local real-time clock in Ada involves calling the function CLOCK provided in the standard package CALENDAR.

11.3.6   Else clauses and terminate alternatives

In addition to waiting selectively for one of several entry calls (or delaying for a timeout) Ada allows the programmer to state that another sequence of statements should be executed if there are no outstanding entry calls on any open accept statements:

```
select
   accept E(...) do
   .
   .
   .
   end E;
else
   <sequence of statements>
end select;
```

Occam does not support this feature directly but it can be constructed using priorities.

The client/server paradigm encourages the programmer, in Ada, to adopt a style of programming in which tasks are either active or passive. Active tasks make entry calls but do not have entries themselves; passive tasks, such as resource controllers and buffers, accept entry calls but do not make them. A common form for a passive task has a select statement positioned within a continuous loop. To make task termination easier, Ada provides a 'terminate' alternative that can be incorporated into a select statement. The effect of this alternative is to terminate the task if there are no more active tasks available to use it, and all other passive tasks are similarly waiting on terminate alternatives. In this situation all passive tasks and their parent will terminate together.

The effect of using a terminate alternative is to reduce the possibility of deadlock at the termination of the program or some subprogram within it. In a section of occam code (i.e. a PAR process) all processes must be instructed to terminate when close-down is required. To achieve this, in the correct order so that neighbours do not finish before all communication has completed, can present a non-trivial problem to occam programmers (see Chapter 6).

11.3.7   Families and replicators

If there is a large number of message sources to choose from, the explicit coding of each alternative becomes long-winded. To deal with a collection of similar message sources Ada provides for a **family** of entries. These are defined with the task specification:

```
task T is
    entry E(0...N)(<entry_parameters>);
end T;
```

and are used either by explicitly writing out each family entry:

```
select
  accept E(0)(...) do
    ...
  end E;
or
  accept E(1)(...) do
    ...
  end E;
or
  accept E(2)(...) do
    ...
  end E;
or
  accept E(3)(...) do
    ...
  end E;
  ...
end select;
```

or in conjunction with a loop statement to analyse the entire family:

```
for i := 0 to N loop
  select
    accept E(i)(...) do
      .
      .
      .
    end E;
  else
    null;
  end select;
end loop;
```

Occam provides a replicator for giving a more concise form:

```
ALT i = 0 FOR N
  ch[i] ? X
    -- process
```

This solution allows an array of channels, of arbitrary length, to be associated with the ALT.

As well as differing in syntax these two approaches also have important semantic differences. The occam model gives equal weight to all the
alternatives and allows the process to be suspended if there are no ready
guards. By comparison, the concise Ada structure polls each of the family
members in turn. The algorithm is not arbitrary and, more significantly,
involves a busy loop if there are no outstanding requests. This is one of the
situations discussed by Gehani and Cargill (1984) in their analysis of the
select statement. They believe that Ada encourages the use of algorithms
that incorporate polling.

11.3.8   Priority

There are situations where the arbitrary nature of the selective wait
statement is not adequate for an algorithm being proposed. Often it is
desirable to give priority over particular alternatives. In Ada this is
achieved by using the **count** attribute which gives the number of outstanding calls there are on any particular entry. Consider a select statement with
three branches:

```
select
  accept HIGH;
or
  when HIGH'count = 0 =>
  accept MID;
or
  when HIGH'count = 0 AND MID'count = 0 =>
  accept LOW;
end select;
```

As well as being verbose for select statements with many alternatives, this
structure is not guaranteed to implement the required priority algorithm.
A high priority task may be in the queue (on the select) when the guards
are evaluated but be aborted (or removed because of a timed entry call –
see next section) before being accepted. The result of this is to close off the
MID and LOW entries even though there is no longer an entry call on HIGH. A
description of a reliable algorithm for Ada is given by Burns (1987).

In recognition of the need to provide a non-arbitrary structure, occam
supports a priority version of the ALT.

11.3.9   Timed and conditional entry calls

There are two ways in which the Ada select statement can be seen to have
more flexibility than the occam ALT. It was noted above that while both
allow a process to wait for one of a number of external calls the Ada
rendezvous allows data to pass in both directions, while the occam

structure is restricted to communication only in the direction of the message. In addition to this, Ada provides a variant of the select statement that allows a task not necessarily, to commit itself to an entry call.

In occam once a process attempts to write to a channel it will be suspended until the appropriate process reads from that channel. Even if this partner process has terminated the writer process will remain suspended. If the corresponding task has terminated, in Ada, an exception will be raised in the caller; this will allow it to continue. Alternatively, if the rendezvous has not yet started, a task can make a conditional or timed entry call. A conditional entry call is cancelled if not immediately accepted; a timed entry call is cancelled if not accepted within a specified time period.

It should, however, be noted that the select statement in Ada is not symmetric; a task cannot select between a number of entry calls, or between a mixture of entry calls and accept statements. These structures can only be programmed by the use of a busy loop containing a number of select statements. The construction of a symmetric select statement for Ada is discussed by Francez and Yemini (1985).

11.4   Programming transactions

It is convenient when considering the interaction between processes to introduce the notion of a **transaction**. A transaction can be defined to be the totality of communication and synchronization necessary to undertake one logical interaction. Neither Ada nor occam directly support transactions. However, one of the motivations for the use of remote invocation in Ada is to code a single logical function as one rendezvous. Unfortunately it has been shown (Burns *et al.*, 1987) that many useful transactions cannot be programmed as a single rendezvous. This is due to the selective wait statement in Ada being based on avoidance rather than condition waiting. Within a monitor a process may start executing a procedure but be suspended if the conditions are not appropriate for completion. A model based on avoidance can prohibit an action from starting, by use of a guard, but has no method of suspending the action once it has commenced.

The guard in Ada does not have access to the 'in' parameters of the entry call. It is therefore necessary in some cases to accept the call in order to ascertain whether the transaction can be accommodated. If it cannot, then the rendezvous must be terminated, and the enquirer asked to call again. Hence a number of transactions require a two-rendezvous algorithm. In occam many more transactions require this double interaction because of the one-directional nature of the communication.

Although the two rendezvous transaction is more common in occam it can, nevertheless, be programmed simply and reliably. This is not the case with Ada (Keeffe *et al.*, 1985). The difficulty arises because nothing can be assumed about the behaviour of the calling task between the two rendezvous. An occam process, given that it makes the second call, is committed to the call. The server task can rely upon it wishing to rendezvous. Due to the existence of the abort statement in Ada a task cannot guarantee to be available for the second rendezvous. Moreover as naming is asymmetric the server cannot, in general, use an exception or an attribute to test for the existence of the client.

The only reliable solution in Ada is to create an anonymous task (called an agent) to undertake the call on behalf of the client. An anonymous task cannot be aborted. This solution unfortunately suffers from storage usage difficulties which necessitate the use of a pool of re-usable agents (Wellings *et al.*, 1984a). Fortunately such agents can be obtained by the application of re-usable generic packages for programming two-rendezvous transactions. However the complexity of the resulting software structure is out of all proportion to the problem being solved. Such structures are unnecessary in occam.

11.5 Programming embedded systems

In both Ada and occam the model of concurrency is extended so that external devices are defined to be processes outside the scope of the program. An interrupt is therefore considered to be a synchronization between an external and an internal process. From the standpoint of the internal process this takes the form of a conventional rendezvous. In Ada the entry that the external process 'calls' when an interrupt occurs is designated by adding a special clause to the entry declaration. A similar construct is used in occam where the channel, down which the interrupt occurs, is mapped onto a predefined address. With both languages the interrupt handler consists of a process that waits for synchronization on the appropriate entry or channel. This process is usually given a high priority.

Where there is a clear difference between the two languages is in their approach to direct communication with hardware. As was discussed earlier there are, in general, two ways in which control information and data can be exchanged with external devices:

- memory mapped registers;
- the provision of special machine code instructions.

Ada caters for both of these approaches by providing a low level input/output package for direct communication with external devices. Alternatively, if this package is not available (which it may not be on all implementations) further facilities are provided. For special instructions, machine code or assembler inserts are allowed within a restricted framework. To facilitate the more common memory mapped input/output,

Ada provides the primitives for constructing and placing objects at designated addresses. The software/hardware communication therefore takes the form of a shared variable interface.

Occam does not allow for machine code inserts although support for PROCs in other languages (i.e. C, Pascal and FORTRAN77) and transputer assembler will be provided. In dealing with the control of external devices occam consistently disallows the use of shared variables. It extends its message based communication model to incorporate memory mapped input/output by the use of ports (see Chapter 9).

11.6 Programming distributed systems

Most programming languages designed with the specific intention of supporting distributed application incorporated the notion of a **virtual node**. A virtual node is an abstraction of a physical node within the distributed system and therefore defines the granularity of distribution (Burns *et al.*, 1987). Communication between virtual nodes is ultimately supported by message passing via the underlying communication subnet. Within a virtual node, if more than one process is allowed, communication may use shared memory.

Occam's processes do not share memory so all that is required to support distribution is a mechanism by which several processes may be associated with one node. This is achieved by the PLACED PAR construct.

The Ada language's philosophy towards distributed programming is not so clear. Although designed with a requirement to be executed on multi-computer systems, the presence of shared memory communication and the lack of a virtual node construct, directly supported by the language, makes distribution difficult.

Two main candidates have been suggested for consideration as virtual nodes in Ada: the task and the package. The task usefulness as a virtual node is limited because it is unable to encapsulate data in the same way as a package, and cannot be a library unit. The Ada package on the other hand is supported by separate compilation, library units, and exception handling facilities. A restricted form of package can be used as a virtual node. Such a package must not allow external access to its variables, and so only task specifications and type declarations may be visible from it. Furthermore, access variables (pointers) may not be declared as parameters to entries. Alternatively, one can restrict the package specifications to contain only procedure declarations, and implement a remote procedure call interface between virtual nodes. In this case one can use tasking to obtain concurrency and synchronization within each virtual node, and use the remote procedure call mechanism for communication between nodes. This model is clearly very different from that of occam.

11.7   Discussion

Although Ada and occam are both concurrent programming languages their representations of parallelism, communication and synchronization are sufficiently different to give rise to two quite distinct languages. As a sequential programming language Ada clearly has a number of features that are superior to those presently available in occam. However, the Ada tasking model is not without its critics, which makes a comparison with occam worth while. Occam provides a much simpler collection of language features, when compared with Ada; it does not support shared variables, aborts, timed or conditional message sends, or an extended rendezvous. Inevitably this results in a language that is less controversial, has a sounder formal base and is more efficiently implementable.

And yet the main distinction between the languages is not what communication features are supported but their differing views as to the nature and notion of a process. In occam the concept of process is fundamental to the structure of the language. An occam program can only be seen as a hierarchy of processes. This is not the case with Ada where the tasking model is, essentially, an addition to a self-contained sequential language.

Appendix A

Reserved Words

The following is a list of the reserved words in occam:

AFTER	PLACE
ALT	PLACED
AND	PLUS
AT	PORT
BITAND	PRI
BITNOT	PROC
BITOR	PROCESSOR
BOOL	REAL
BYTE	REAL32
CASE	REAL64
CHAN	RECORD
ELSE	REM
FALSE	RESULT
FOR	RETYPES
FROM	ROUND
FUNCTION	SEQ
IF	SIZE
INT	SKIP
INT16	STOP
INT32	TIMER
INT64	TIMES
IS	TRUE
MINUS	TRUNC
MOSTNEG	TYPE
MOSTPOS	VAL
NOT	VALOF
OF	WHILE
OR	WORKSPACE
PAR	

The Syntax of Occam 2

B.1 Top-down description

The following is a top-down description of the syntax of occam 2. In this description *{process}* means zero or more processes on separate lines; *{₁, object}* means one or more objects separated by commas; and *{₀; object}* means zero or more objects separated by, on this occasion, semicolon. The symbol | means 'or'; and = is a metasymbol apart from its use in the definition of a replicator.

```
process =   SKIP
          | STOP
          | action
          | construction
          | block
          | instance
          | CASE selector
              {selection}


action =   assignment
         | input
         | case input
         | output


assignment =   variable := expression
             | variable list := expression list


variable list = {₁ , variable}


expression list =   {₁ , expression}
                  | (valof
                    )
                  | name({₀ , expression})
```

```
input =    channel ? input item
        |  channel ? {1 , input item}
        |  channel ? CASE tagged list
        |  timer ? variable
        |  timer ? AFTER expression
        |  port ? variable

input item =   variable
            |  variable :: variable

case input = channel ? CASE
                {variant}

guarded case input = boolean & channel ? CASE
                         {variant}

variant =   tagged list
               process
         |  specification
               variant

tagged list =   tag
             |  tag ; {1 ; input item}

tag = name

output =   channel ! output item
        |  channel ! {1 ; output item}
        |  channel ! tag
        |  channel ! tag ; {1 ; output item}
        |  port ! expression

output item =   expression
             |  expression :: expression

variable = element

channel = element

timer = element

port = element

construction =   loop
              |  conditional
              |  sequence
              |  parallel
              |  alteration
```

```
loop = WHILE boolean
         process

boolean = expression

conditional =   IF
                   {choice}
               | IF replicator
                   choice

choice =   guarded choice
         | conditional
         | specification
           choice

guarded choice = boolean
                   process

replicator = name = base FOR count

base = expression

count = expression

sequence =   SEQ
               {process}
           | SEQ replicator
               process

parallel =   PAR
               {process}
           | PAR replicator
               process
           | PLACED PAR
               {placement}
           | PLACED PAR replicator
               placement
           | PRI PAR
               {process}
           | PRI PAR replicator
               process

placement = PROCESSOR expression
              process

alternation =   ALT
                   {alternative}
               | ALT replicator
```

```
                              alternative
                          |   PRI ALT
                              {alternative}
                          |   PRI ALT replicator
                              alternative

        alternative =     guarded alternative
                          |   alternation
                          |   case input
                          |   guarded case input
                          |   specification
                              alternative

        guarded alternative = guard
                                    process

        guard =     input
                    |   boolean & input
                    |   boolean & SKIP

        block =     specification
                    scope
                    |   allocation
                    scope

        specification =   declaration
                          |   abbreviation
                          |   definition

        scope = process

        declaration = type name:

        type =    primitive type
                  |   PORT OF type
                  |   array type
                  |   record type

        primitive type =    CHAN OF protocol
                            |   TIMER
                            |   BOOL
                            |   BYTE
                            |   INT
                            |   REAL32
                            |   REAL64
                            |   REAL
                            |   INT16
                            |   INT32
                            |   INT64
```

```
protocol =   name
           | simple protocol
           | ANY


array type = [expression]type


record type = ({₁ , type})


abbreviation =   specifier name IS element:
               | VAL specifier name IS expression:


specifier =   primitive type
            | [expression]specifier
            | []specifier


definition =   specifier name RETYPES element:
             | VAL specifier name RETYPES expression:
             | TYPE name IS type:
             | RECORD name IS record type:
             | PROC name ({₀ , formal})
                  body
               :
             | {₁ , type}FUNCTION name({₀ , formal}) IS expression list:
             | {₁ , type}FUNCTION name({₀ , formal})
                  function body
               :
             | PROTOCOL name IS simple protocol:
             | PROTOCOL name IS sequential protocol:
             | PROTOCOL name
                  CASE
                     {tagged protocol}
               :


formal =   specifier name
         | VAL specifier name


body = process


function body = valof


valof =   VALOF
             process
             RESULT expression list
        | specification
          valof
```

```
simple protocol =   type
                  | type::[]type


sequential protocol = {1 ; simple protocol}


tagged protocol =   tag
                  | tag ; protocol


allocation =   PLACE name AT expression:


instance = name ({0 , actual})


actual =   element
         | expression


selector =   expression


selection =   expression
                  process
            | ELSE
                  process


element =   element[subscript]
          | [element FROM subscript FOR subscript]
          | [{,element}]
          | ({,element})
          | name


subscript = expression


expression =   monadic.operator operand
             | operand dyadic.operator operand
             | conversion
             | operand
             | MOSTPOS type
             | MOSTNEG type


operand =   element
          | literal
          | [{1 , expression}]
          | ({1 , expression})
          | (expression)
          | name({0 , expression})
          | ( valof
            )
```

```
literal =    integer
         | byte
         | integer(type)
         | byte(type)
         | real(type)
         | string
         | TRUE
         | FALSE


integer =    digits
         | #digits


byte = 'character'


real =    digits.digits
      | digits.digitsEexponent


exponent =    +digits
          | -digits


conversion =    type operand
            | type ROUND operand
            | type TRUNC operand


monadic.operator = - | NOT | SIZE


dyadic.operator =    + | - | * | / | REM | PLUS | MINUS
                 | TIMES | /\ | \/ | >< | >> | << |~
                 | AND | OR | = | <> | < | > | <= | >=


alphabetic.characters ARE abcdefghijklmnopqrstuvwxyz
                          ABCDEFGHIJKLMNOPQRSTUVWXYZ


digits ARE 0123456789


special.characters ARE ! " # & ' ( ) * + , - . / : ; < = > ? [ ] AND
space character


A string can contain alphabetical.characters, digits and
special.characters (apart from *, ' AND ").


A name consists of a sequence of alphabetic.characters,
digits and dot (.), the first must be an alphabetic.character.
```

B.2   Alphabetical definition of the syntax

```
abbreviation =   specifier name IS element:
               | VAL specifier name IS expression:


action =   assignment
         | input
         | case input
         | output


actual =   element
         | expression


allocation =   PLACE name AT expression:


alternation =   ALT
                   {alternative}
              | ALT replicator
                   alternative
              | PRI ALT
                   {alternative}
              | PRI ALT replicator
                   alternative


alternative =   guarded alternative
              | alternation
              | case input
              | guarded case input
              | specification
                alternative


array type = [expression]type


assignment =   variable := expression
             | variable list := expression list


base = expression


block =   specification
          scope
        | allocation
          scope


body = process


boolean = expression
```

```
byte = 'character'

case input = channel ? CASE
                {variant}

channel = element

choice =   guarded choice
         | conditional
         | specification
           choice

conditional =   IF
                  {choice}
              | IF replicator
                  choice

construction =   loop
               | conditional
               | sequence
               | parallel
               | alteration

conversion =   type operand
             | type ROUND operand
             | type TRUNC operand

count = expression

declaration = type name:

definition =   specifier name RETYPES element:
             | VAL specifier name RETYPES expression:
             | TYPE name IS type:
             | RECORD name IS record type:
             | PROC name ({0 , formal})
                 body
               :
             | {1 , type}FUNCTION name({0 , formal}) IS expression list:
             | {1 , type}FUNCTION name({0 , formal})
                 function body
               :
             | PROTOCOL name IS simple protocol:
             | PROTOCOL name IS sequential protocol:
             | PROTOCOL name
                 CASE
                   {tagged protocol}
               :
```

```
dyadic.operator =   + | - | * | / | REM | PLUS | MINUS
                  | TIMES | /\ | \/ | >< | >> | << | ~
                  | AND | OR | = | <> | < | > | <= | >=

element =   element[subscript]
          | [element FROM subscript FOR subscript]
          | [{,element}]
          | ({,element})
          | name

exponent =   + digits
           | - digits

expression =   monadic.operator operand
             | operand dyadic.operator operand
             | conversion
             | operand
             | MOSTPOS type
             | MOSTNEG type

expression list =   {1 , expression}
                  | (valof
                    )
                  | name({0 , expression})

formal =   specifier name
         | VAL specifier name

function body = valof

guard =   input
        | boolean & input
        | boolean & SKIP

guarded alternative = guard
                          process

guarded case input = Boolean & channel ? CASE
                         {variant}

guarded choice = Boolean
                    process

input =   channel ? input item
        | channel ? {1 , input item}
        | channel ? CASE tagged list
        | timer ? variable
        | timer ? AFTER expression
        | port ? variable
```

```
input item =   variable
             | variable :: variable

instance = name ({₀ , actual})

integer =   digits
          | #digits

literal =   integer
          | byte
          | integer(type)
          | byte(type)
          | real(type)
          | string
          | TRUE
          | FALSE

loop = WHILE Boolean
         process

monadic.operator = - | NOT | SIZE

operand =   element
          | literal
          | [{₁, expression}]
          | ({₁, expression})
          | (expression)
          | name({₀, expression})
          | ( valof
                    )

output =   channel ! output item
         | channel ! {₁ ; output item}
         | channel ! tag
         | channel ! tag ; {₁ ; output item}
         | port ! expression

output item =   expression
              | expression :: expression

parallel =   PAR
               {process}
           | PAR replicator
               process
           | PLACED PAR
               {placement}
           | PLACED PAR replicator
               placement
           | PRI PAR
               {process}
```

```
              | PRI PAR replicator
                process

placement = PROCESSOR expression
                process

port = element

primitive type =   CHAN OF protocol
                 | TIMER
                 | BOOL
                 | BYTE
                 | INT
                 | REAL32
                 | REAL64
                 | REAL
                 | INT16
                 | INT32
                 | INT64

process =   SKIP
          | STOP
          | action
          | construction
          | block
          | instance
          | CASE selector
               {selection}

protocol =   name
           | simple protocol
           | ANY

real =   digits.digits
       | digits.digitsEexponent

record type = ({1 , type})

replicator = name = base FOR count

scope = process

selection =   expression
                process
            | ELSE
                process

selector =   expression
```

```
sequence =   SEQ
                {process}
           | SEQ replicator
                process

sequential protocol = {1 ; simple protocol}

simple protocol =   type
                  | type::[]type

specification =   declaration
                | abbreviation
                | definition

specifier =   primitive type
            | [expression]specifier
            | []specifier

subscript = expression

tag = name

tagged list =   tag
              | tag ; {1 ; input item}

tagged protocol =   tag
                  | tag ; protocol

timer = element

type =   primitive type
       | PORT of type
       | array type
       | record type

valof =   VALOF
             process
             RESULT expression list
        | specification
          valof

variable = element

variable list = {1 , variable}

variant =   tagged list
               process
          | specification
            variant
```

Appendix C

Representation of Reals

A value of type REAL32 or REAL64 is represented according to ANSI/IEEE standard 754–1985. For a value of type REAL32 this means that there is an 8-bit exponent, e, and a 23-bit fraction, f. The value, v, is positive if the sign bit is equal to 0; otherwise it is negative. Its magnitude is given by:

```
(2**(e - 127)) * 1.f      if 0 < e and e < 255
(2** - 126) * 0.f         if e = 0 and f <> 0
0                         if e = 0 and f = 0
```

A value is effectively infinity if $e = 255$ and $f = 0$. Alternatively it is not a number if $e = 255$ and f has any value other than 0.

With type REAL64, a value has an 11-bit exponent and a 52-bit fraction. The corresponding magnitudes are:

```
(2**(e - 1023)) * 1.f     if 0 < e and e < 2047
(2** - 1022) * 0.f        if e = 0 and f <> 0
0                        if e = 0 and f = 0
infinity                 if e = 2047 and f = 0
not a number             if e = 2047 and f <> 0
```

The result of a real arithmetic expression, e, is the value of e rounded to the nearest value of the appropriate real type. If x any y are real then the result of xREMy is $x - (y * n)$ where n is the result of x / y rounded to the nearest integer value.

Appendix D

Predefined Procedures

The following are predefined arithmetic procedures that provide fractional multiplication, arithmetic shifts, word rotations and the primitives to construct multiple length integer arithmetic and multiple length shift operations. They are provided as standard with the transputer's occam development system.

LONGADD	signed addition with a carry in.
LONGSUM	unsigned addition with a carry in and a carry out.
LONGSUB	signed subtraction with a borrow in.
LONGDIFF	unsigned subtraction with a borrow in and a borrow out.
LONGPROD	unsigned multiplication with a carry in, producing a double length result.
LONGDIV	unsigned division of a double length number, producing a single length result.
SHIFTRIGHT	right shift on a double length quantity.
SHIFTLEFT	left shift on a double length quantity.
NORMALIZE	normalize a double length quantity.
ASHIFTRIGHT	arithmetic right shift on a double length quantity.
ASHIFTLEFT	arithmetic left shift on a double length quantity.
ROTATERIGHT	rotate a word right.
ROTATELEFT	rotate a word left.

Earlier Versions of Occam

If this is occam 2 there must have been an occam 1! (In fact not only was there occam 1 but before that, there was a preliminary occam.) It may, therefore, be of interest to the reader briefly to describe the earlier version of the language and to consider why it had to change (i.e. expand). In terms of the language described in this book, occam 1 had the following restrictions:

1. It did not support floating point representations.
2. It only supported one dimensional arrays.
3. It did not contain records.
4. It would only allow one object to be communicated per rendezvous.
5. It had no concept of abbreviation and the parameter passing model was less well defined.
6. It had no functions.
7. Access to the real-time clock was achieved in a manner at variance with the basic model (it used a one-to-many channel).

Essentially occam 1 was a language that had only a single data type. Objects were defined to be VARs (variables) and were usually accessed as integers although Boolean and character interpretations were allowed.

On these peripheral aspects of the languages occam 1 and occam 2 are quite distinct. However, the core language features are almost identical. The basic process model is the same, as are the primitive processes and the constructors. It has therefore not been difficult for the programmers who were familiar with the original language to adapt to occam 2.

Occam 1 was never meant to be a final version of the language as its functionality did not meet the capabilities of the transputer. In particular the transputer could support:

- floating point representation;
- block memory transfer on a single processor;
- block memory transfers, via a link, from memory on one transputer to memory on another.

Occam 2 has been designed to allow the programmer to utilize these features.

Perhaps the greatest difficulty that the new features presented was to design a concise syntax for communicating objects of different size and type down the same channel. In occam 1 all channels passed single, word long, objects; there was no need to specify a type or protocol with the channel. Occam 2's type model has necessitated the addition of a protocol field; the syntactical form of which took a number of design interactions to get to the version that is described in this book.

In the Introduction it was described how the name occam had been chosen because the language was no more complicated than was absolutely necessary. This was certainly true with occam 1 whose definition fitted on to one side of A4 paper. Occam 2 will still fit on to one piece of paper; but the printing is a little smaller!

Bibliography

Ada Reference Manual, Ichbiah, J. (1983). 'Reference Manual for the Ada Programming Language', ANSI/MIL-STD-1815A

Andrews, G.R. (1982).'The Distributed Programming Language SR – Mechanisms, Design and Implementation' *Software – Practice and Experience*, **12**(8), 719–754

Andrews, G.R. and Schneider, F.B. (1983). 'Concepts and Notations for Concurrent Programming' *Computer Surveys*, **15**(1), 3–43

Apt, K.R., Francez, N., and deRoever, W.P. (1980). 'A Proof System for Communicating Sequential Processes' *ACM Transactions on Programming Languages and Systems*, **2**(3), 359–385

Barnes, J.G.P. (1984). *Programming in Ada*. Wokingham: Addison-Wesley, second edition

Barron, I.M. (1978). 'The Transputer' In *Microprocessor and its Applications*. Cambridge: Cambridge University Press, 343–357

Ben-Ari, M. (1982). *Principles of Concurrent Programming*. Englewood Cliffs, NJ: Prentice-Hall

Brinch Hansen, P. (1972). 'Structured Multi-Programming' *CACM*, **15**(7), 574–578

Brinch Hansen, P. (1973 a). *Concurrent Programming Concepts ACM Computer Surveys*, **5**(4), 223–245

Brinch Hansen, P. (1973 b). *Operating System Principles*. Englewood Cliffs, NJ: Prentice-Hall

Brinch Hansen, P. (1975). 'The Programming Language Concurrent Pascal' *IEEE Trans. Software Engng*, **2**, 199–207

Brinch Hansen, P. (1978). 'Distributed Processes: A Concurrent Programming Concept' *CACM*, **21**(11), 934–941

Brinch Hansen, P. (1981). 'Edison: a Multi-Processor Language' *Software – Practice and Experience*, **11**(4), 325–361

Brookes, S.D., Hoare, C.A.R., and Roscoe, A.W. (1984). 'A Theory of Communicating Sequential Processes' *Journal of the ACM*, **31**(3), 560–599

Buckley, G.N. and Silberschatz, A. (1983). 'An Effective Implementation for the Generalized Input-Output Construct of CSP' *ACM Transactions on Programming Languages and Systems*, **5**(2), 223–235

Burns, A. (1985). *Concurrent Programming in Ada*, Ada Companion Series. Cambridge: Cambridge University Press

Burns, A., (1987). 'Using Large Families for Handling Priority Requests' *Ada Letters*, **7**(1), 97–104

Burns, A., Lister, A.M., and Wellings, A.J. (1987). *A Review of Ada Tasking, Lecture Notes in Computer Science*. Berlin: Springer-Verlag

Cook, R.P. (1979). '*MOD – A Language for Distributed Programming' *Proc 1st Int. Conf on Distributed Computing Systems*, Huntsville, Alabama. 233–241

Dijkstra, E.W. (1968 a) 'Cooperating Sequential Processes' In Genuys, F.; Ed. *Programming Languages*. London: ACPRESS

Dijkstra, E.W. (1986 b). 'The Structure of "THE" Multi-Programming System' *CACM*, **11**(5), 341–346

Dijkstra, E.W. (1971). 'Hierarchichial Ordering of Sequential Processes' *ACTA*, **1**, 115–138

Dijkstra, E.W. (1975). 'Guarded Commands, Nondeterminancy and Formal Derivation of Programs' *CACM*, **18**(8), 453–457

Fay, D.Q.M. (1984). 'Comparison of CSP and the Programming Language Occam' *Australian Computer Science Communications* **6**(1)

Fay, D.Q.M. (1985). 'Interrupts and the Hardware Software Rendezvous' *Microprocessors and Microsystems*, **9**(2), 57–63

Francez, N. and Yemini, A. (1985). 'Symmetric Intertask Communication' *ACM Transactions on Programming Languages and Systems* **7**(4), 622–636

Gehani, N.H. (1984). *Ada Concurrent Programming*. Englewood Cliffs, NJ: Prentice-Hall

Gehani, N.H. and Cargill, T.A. (1984). 'Concurrent Programming in the Ada Language: the Polling Bias' *Software – Practice and Experience*, **14**(5), 413–427

Gentleman, W.M. (1978). 'Some Complexity Results for Matrix Computation on Parallel Processors' *Journal of ACM*, **25**, 112–115

Hoare, C.A.R. (1972). 'Towards a Theory of Parallel Programming' In Perrott, R.H.; Ed. *Operating System Techniques*. ACPRESS

Hoare, C.A.R. (1974). 'Monitors: an Operating System Structuring Concept' *CACM*, **17**(10), 549–557

Hoare, C.A.R. (1978). 'Communicating Sequential Processes' *CACM*, **21**(8), 666–677

Hoare, C.A.R. (1981 a). 'The Emperor's New Clothes (1980 ACM Turing Award Lecture)' *Communications of the ACM*, **24**(2), 75–83

Hoare, C.A.R. (1981 b). 'A Calculus for Total Correctness for Communicating Sequential Processes' *Science of Computer Programming*, **1**, 49–72

Hoare, C.A.R. (1985). *Communicating Sequential Processes*. Englewood Cliffs, NJ: Prentice-Hall

Ichbiah, J.D., Barnes, J.G.P., Firth, R.J., and Woodger, M. (1979). 'Rationale for the Design of the Green Programming Language'. Minneapolis: Honeywell, Inc. and Cii Honeywell Bull

INMOS Limited (1984). *Occam Programming Manual*. London: Prentice-Hall

INMOS Limited (1987). *Occam 2 Product Definition (Preliminary)*. Bristol: INMOS

Jones, C.B., (1983). 'Specification and Design of Parallel Programs' *Proc of IFIP 83*, 321–332, North-Holland

Keeffe, D., Tomlinson, G.M., Wand, I.C., and Wellings, A.J. (1985). *PULSE – an Ada-based Unix-like Distributed Operating System*. Orlanda: Academic Press

Kennaway, J.R. and Hoare C.A.R. (1980). 'A Theory of Nondeterminism' *Lecture Notes in Computer Science*, (85), 338–350. Berlin: Springer-Verlag

Kung, H.T. (1982). 'Why Systolic Architectures' *IEEE Computing*, **15**, 37–46

Lamport, L. (1983). 'Specifying Concurrent Program Modules' *TOPLAS*, **5**(2), 190–222

Lehmann, D., Pnueli, A., and Stavi, J. (1981). 'Impartiality, Justice and Fairness: The Ethics of Concurrent Termination' *Automata, Languages and Programming, Lecture Notes in Computer Science*, **115**, 264–277. Berlin: Springer-Verlag

Liskov, B.L. (1982). 'On Linguistic Support for Distributed Programs' *Proc IEEE Symp Reliability in Distributed Systems and Data-base Systems*, 53–60. New York: IEEE

Liskov, B.L. and Scheifler, R. (1983). 'Guardians and Actions: Linguistic Support for Robust, Distributed Programs' *TOPLAS*, **5**(3), 381–404

May, D. (1983). 'Occam' *ACM SIGPLAN Notices*, **18**(4), 69–79,

May, D. (1986). *Communicating Processes and occam*. Bristol: INMOS

May, D. and Keane, C. (1986). *Compiling occam into Silicon*. Bristol: INMOS

May, D. and Shepherd, R. (1984). 'Occam and the Transputer' *Proc IFIP Workshop on Hardware Supported Implementation of Concurrent Languages in Distributed Systems*, Univ. of Bristol, UK, March 26–28.

May, D. and Shepherd, R. (1986 a). *The Transputer Implementation of occam*. Bristol: INMOS

May, D. and Shepherd, R. (1986 b). *Communicating Process Computers*. Bristol: INMOS

May, D. and Taylor, R. (1984). 'Occam – an Overview' *Microprocessors and Microsystems*, **8**(2), 73–79

Newport, J.R. (1986). 'An Introduction to occam and the Development of Parallel Software' *Software Engineering Journal*, **1**, 165–169

Roscoe, A.W. (1985). 'Denotational Semantics for occam' *Lecture Notes in Computer Science*, **197**. Berlin: Springer-Verlag

Roscoe, A.W. and Hoare C.A.R. (1986) 'The Laws of occam Programming' *Oxford University Programming Research Group*, **PRG–53**

Samwell, P.M. (1986). 'Experience with occam for Simulating Systolic and Wavefront Arrays' *Software Engineering Journal*, **1**(5), 196–204

Schonberg, E. and Schonberg, E. (1985). 'Highly Parallel Ada – Ada on an Ultracomputer' *Ada in use, Proc of the Ada Int. Conf, Paris*. Cambridge: Cambridge University Press

Wellings, A.J. (1985). 'The Use of Ada Tasking in the Implementation of a Distributed Operating System' *Ada UK News*, **6**(3), 53–60

Wellings, A.J., Keeffe, D., and Tomlinson, G.M. (1984 a). 'A Problem with Ada and Resource Allocation' *Ada Letters*, **3**(4)

Wellings, A.J., Tomlinson, G.M, Keeffe, D. and Wand, I.C. (1984 b). 'Communication between Ada Programs' *Proc of the IEEE Conference on Ada Applications and Environments*, St. Paul Minnesota. 145–152

Welsh, J. and Bustard, D.W. (1979). 'Pascal-Plus – Another Language for Modular Multiprogramming' *Software – Practice and Experience*, **9**, 947–957

Welsh, J. and Lister A.M (1981). 'A Comparative Study of Task Communication in Ada' *Software – Practice and Experience*, **11**(3), 257–290

Wirth, N. (1977). 'Modula: a Language for Modular Multiprogramming' *Software – Practice and Experience*, **7**, 3–35

Wirth, N. (1982). *Programming in Modula-2*. Springer-Verlag

Yemini, S. (1982). 'On the Suitability of Ada Multi-Tasking for Expressing Parallel Algorithms' *Proc of the AdaTec Conf on Ada*, Arlington, pp. 91–97

Young, S.J. (1982) *Real Time Languages*. Chichester: Ellis Horwood

Index